PENGUIN BOOKS

A CHURCHILL FAMILY ALBUM

Mary Soames was born in 1922, the youngest of Winston and Clementine Churchill's five children. She was brought up at Chartwell, attending a local private school as a day-pupil until 1939. During the first two years of the war she worked for the Red Cross and the W.V.S., and in 1941 she joined the A.T.S. She served in mixed anti-aircraft batteries, mainly in the United Kingdom, but also in Belgium and Germany, rising through the ranks to a commission and the eventual rank of Junior Commander. She also accompanied her father on several of his overseas journeys, acting as his A.D.C.

Demobilized in 1946, she married Captain Christopher Soames of the Coldstream Guards, who was at that time Assistant Military Attaché in Paris. After leaving the army he became Conservative M.P. for Bedford from 1950 to 1966, and Mary Soames campaigned with her husband at six elections. Having held several government posts and attained Cabinet rank, Christopher Soames was sent to Paris as British Ambassador, where he and his wife and family lived from 1968 to 1972. In 1973, Sir Christopher was appointed first British Vice-President of the European Commission, and until 1976 he and Lady Soames lived in Brussels. From December 1979 to April 1980 Lady Soames accompanied her husband on his appointment as the last British Governor of Southern Rhodesia. Lord and Lady Soames have five children.

Mary Soames was United Kingdom Chairman of the International Year of the Child in 1979; she is a member of the Council of the Winston Churchill Memorial Trust; a Governor of Harrow School, and an Honorary Fellow of Churchill College, Cambridge. In 1980 she was made a Dame Commander of the Order of the British Empire. She likes reading, travelling and sightseeing and – above all – family life, living in the country and gardening. Mary Soames is also author of *Clementine Churchill*, the best-selling biography of her mother, which won a Wolfson History Prize and the *Yorkshire Post* Prize for Best First Work in 1979.

A CHURCHILL FAMILY ALBUM

A personal anthology selected by
MARY SOAMES

PENGUIN BOOKS

Penguin Books Ltd, Harmondsworth, Middlesex, England
Viking Penguin Inc., 40 West 23rd Street, New York, New York 10010, U.S.A.
Penguin Books Australia Ltd, Ringwood, Victoria, Australia
Penguin Books Canada Ltd, 2801 John Street, Markham, Ontario, Canada L3R 1B4
Penguin Books (N.Z.) Ltd, 182–190 Wairau Road, Auckland 10, New Zealand

First published by Allen Lane 1982
Published in Penguin Books 1985

Made and printed in Great Britain by Lund Humphries Ltd, Bradford
Typeset in Palatino

Frontispiece

Winston and Clementine Churchill at Chartwell:
the sketch for the conversation piece by William Nicholson,
commissioned by a group of their friends
to mark their Silver Wedding in 1933. The picture hangs at Chartwell.

Contents

To my grandchildren

Foreword

All family albums seem to have a fascination for succeeding generations; nor does 'the family' have to be famous for the events and people pictured in the faded sepia prints, or the stylised studio portraits and snapshots, to be interesting or amusing: 'Were hats *really* like that Mama?' Or, looking at some dear little person in velvet frills: 'Is that *really* Uncle Henry?' On how many wet afternoons, promised picnics abandoned, have children been consoled and kept blissfully quiet for hours, turning the pages of old scrapbooks and albums? And not only children – the world of yesterday and the day before, can hold grown-up attention too, leaving the TV talking to itself.

The lives of my parents, Winston and Clementine Churchill, spanned just over a century: both born in the twilight of the Victorian age, they were to see five more sovereigns on the throne of England; they witnessed the bitter colonial tussle of the Boer War; were part of the heated political battles of the first decade of the new century; and they lived the convulsions of the two holocausts that have darkened our times – the First World War sweeping away an entire generation of young men, and both unleashing political and social changes which rock us still. My parents were not unique in this – all those who shared all or part of that troubled century could make the same claim. But Winston and Clementine's lives have an added dimension – from early manhood onwards, Winston began to be seen as one of the dramatis personae of the unfolding pageant of the times; and from their marriage in 1908 for the next fifty-seven years, Clementine was to be at his side. Their life together evokes memories and emotions for countless people who never even knew them, but saw them moving on the brightly lit stage of their public life, and who trace in Winston and Clementine's lives the public events and dramas which have also marked their own.

Winston Churchill is likely to remain a commanding historical figure: and even now, seventeen years after his death, worldwide interest is still shown, not only in his public and political activities, but also in his private life, and in the circumstances and strands which composed so remarkable a human personality. It is this interest which has encouraged me to make this present book – compiling it in the manner of a family album.

Turning the pages of old photograph books, albums and scrapbooks, or sorting through battered old box files and dress boxes of photographs, menus, theatre programmes, newspaper cuttings, odd poems, cartoons, letters and old Christmas cards, has been rivetting employment for me. And I have laughed, and I have felt the excitement of bygone days, and sometimes I have cried too, as I dredged up our family's past. At times I have felt with Swinburne that 'time remembered is grief forgotten'. And sometimes, when I find the fragments of griefs and hurts beyond repair or recall, I cry with Tennyson:

'O Death in Life, the days that are no more'.

I have elsewhere made acknowledgement to those who have helped me in various ways, and also made material available to me, and the provenance of every picture is listed. But the main sources from which I have compiled this book have been my mother's albums; my own scrapbooks and albums; and various other family collections. My mother was a somewhat haphazard 'albumeer', and the chronology is very erratic; but her collections of some eight unwieldy volumes is a rich treasure trove. She also possessed various presentation albums of special occasions, and many wartime (1939-45) photographs come from albums of official photographs in her possession. I started keeping a scrapbook in 1939 when I was seventeen, and there are now over eighteen volumes of highly personalized 'hotchpotch'. In these last few years, I have also made a wider collection of material concerning my parents' lives, started when I was writing my mother's biography (published in 1979). Other family collections which have been invaluable to me are my sister, Sarah Audley's collection; the Broadwater Collection (my father's own collection, now the property of my nephew, Winston Churchill); my first cousin Peregrine Churchill's family albums; and my cousin the Duke of Marlborough's collection at Blenheim.

Finally, I must emphasize that this book is essentially a personal anthology. It does not seek to be a pictorial history of our times – although history is here, and politics too – barging in as they so often did on our family life, and asserting their own over-riding priorities. It is not even a complete *family* history: it is simply *my* choice of pictures and memorabilia: some of the photographs may be familiar, some quite new – but they are all chosen because I like them, and because I think they show Winston and Clementine Churchill, not so much 'at their best', but as I found or saw them to be, at times of their lives and in situations which are highlighted for me in some way or another. As I have turned back the pages of their truly remarkable lives, I am conscious that others too may be looking over my shoulder, and I have tried to fill some gaps, and to show something of our private family life, and the people who played their part in our domestic scene or were my father's colleagues and companions.

I am blessed with too full and happy a life to want to live in the past, however glowing and glorious: but I like to visit it from time to time – and this is what I have done in this book.

Acknowledgements

I would like to thank Stanley Glazer, who has designed the book, and John Taylor of Lund Humphries Publishers Ltd for all their enthusiasm and patience at every stage of its compilation: it has been a great pleasure to work with them. I am greatly indebted also to Vanessa Whinney who has done the picture research, tracked down sources of pictures, and found many 'missing links' for me.

Much of the material in this book is drawn from my own albums and collections of photographs, etc: The Mary Soames Collection. The provenance of every picture and the copyright-holders (where known) are all listed on page 220, but I would like to make the following special acknowledgements: I have used much material from my mother's own collection, The Baroness Spencer-Churchill Collection, which is owned by the Sunday Times/Thomson Trust, and I am most grateful to the Trustees for permission to use this material, which formed the basis of my mother's biography *Clementine Churchill by her daughter Mary Soames* published by Cassell in 1979. I want to thank my husband Christopher, for much helpful criticism and advice, and for lending me photographs of his own. My sister, Sarah Audley, allowed me to hunt through her own large collection of photographs and cuttings, and I am so grateful to her, and also for her encouragement and help on many matters. My thanks to my nephew Winston Churchill, for allowing me to reproduce the portrait of my father by Sir William Orpen, and also for permitting me to have access to The Broadwater Collection (my father's own collection of photographs, now in his possession, but held by Churchill College, Cambridge). I am greatly indebted to my first cousin Peregrine Churchill, for allowing me full access to his family albums. And I wish to thank my cousin, the Duke of Marlborough, for allowing me to use pictures from his personal collection of photographs at Blenheim Palace, and for allowing me also to use a facsimile page from the Blenheim Visitors' Book.

I want to record my gratitude to the Master and Fellows of Churchill College, Cambridge, and to Correlli Barnett, Keeper of Archives, for allowing me and my colleagues full access to The Broadwater Collection and to the Churchill College Press Photograph Collection. I am also extremely grateful to Marion Stewart, Archivist, and to Alan Kucia, Assistant Archivist, for all the time and trouble they have given to helping us with matters concerning the book; and to Peter Lofts for copying photographs for us.

I am indebted to the Administrative Trustees of the Chequers Estate and Her Majesty's Stationery Office for permission to use photographs of Chequers and I want to thank also Vera E. Thomas O.B.E., Wing-Commander W.R.A.F. (Retd), the Curator at Chequers for her assistance. I am most grateful to Sir Philip Adams K.C.M.G., the Director at Ditchley, for his help in searching out photographs from the collection there, and to the Trustees of the Ditchley Foundation for permission to use them. I am grateful to the Syndics of the Fitzwilliam Museum for permission to use the photograph of my mother with her first baby. I am particularly indebted to John Frost for all his help in finding for us newspaper cuttings and whole pages from his remarkable John Frost Historical Newspaper Collection. I am grateful to the Trustees of the Imperial War Museum, London for permission to reproduce many photographs in their copyright; and I want to thank especially members of the Department of Photographs for their assistance. The National Trust at Chartwell have been most generous in allowing me to reproduce several pictures at Chartwell; and I want also to thank Mrs Jean Broome, the Administrator at Chartwell for her ever ready help.

The following individuals have most kindly made photographs or other material available to me, and I am most grateful to them: Viscount Camrose; Mrs Thelma Cazalet-Keir; Sir John Colville, C.B., C.V.O.; Viscountess Head; Mary, Duchess of Roxburghe; and Hugo Vickers.

I am grateful to Miss Ann Hoffman of Authors' Research Services who answered several tricky queries and to Miss Grace Hamblin, O.B.E., for helping me to track down various family photographs. And I also want to thank my secretary Mrs Judy Meisenkothen, for her invaluable help at all times.

We have in all cases diligently tried to verify the sources and copyright-holders of all the material used in this book: but this has often proved extremely difficult, and sometimes even impossible, where photographs either bear no clue to their attribution, or have been pasted down in the various albums and scrapbooks. We apologize for any omissions or errors therefore which may have been inadvertently committed.

The young Winston

1

This infant is Winston Leonard Spencer Churchill. He was born into the privileged world of the British aristocracy in the last quarter of the nineteenth century: the scion of a noble house, and a descendant of John, 1st Duke of Marlborough, whose victories against Britain's enemies in the early seventeenth century had won him lasting fame in history, and a grandiose monument in Blenheim Palace – to proclaim to succeeding generations not only Marlborough's feat of arms, but also the glories of the reign of Queen Anne, to which they had added so lasting a lustre. Yet this illustrious heritage bore no guarantee to this child of either wealth, place or a lasting name: his father, a brilliant but ephemeral politician, was the younger son of the 7th Duke of Marlborough, and the lion's share of the encumbered family fortunes were destined for his elder brother, the heir to the Dukedom and Blenheim. Winston's beautiful American mother brought no great fortune, but a more precious gift – the infusion of vigorous blood and a sturdy constitution. Yet nothing in his childhood or youth pointed to Winston Churchill's diverse talents or to the destiny which awaited him. His life would span two eras: as a young man he would ride in the last cavalry charge of history; after entering politics, and years of fluctuating fortunes, his finest hour would also be Britain's. Hailed as his country's saviour, he was to live on to a vigorous old age, and attend upon the dawning of the nuclear age.

2

Lord Randolph Churchill, the younger son of the 7th Duke of Marlborough, and Jennie Jerome,
one of the three beautiful daughters of Leonard Jerome and Clara Hall Jerome
of New York City, were married in Paris in April 1874. Although she was born in Brooklyn,
Jennie, from the age of four, had been brought up in Paris, where
her mother preferred to live, while Mr Jerome remained in New York, and
made (and lost) a fortune or two. Randolph and Jennie had met during Cowes Week
in August 1873 – he was twenty-four, Jennie nineteen – and it was love at
first sight. Both sets of parents, for differing reasons, opposed the match, but
their objections were overruled by the young people's determination.

3

Jennie (above left) with her elder and younger sisters – Clara and Leonie. The Jerome girls were renowned for their beauty, charm and cultivation. Having been brought up and educated in Paris, they spoke without a trace of an American accent. Jennie in particular was outstandingly beautiful and lively. She spoke excellent French, and played the piano and sang with real talent. Randolph's father, the Duke of Marlborough, was appointed Viceroy of Ireland in 1877. Randolph and Jennie accompanied his parents to Dublin, where Randolph acted as his father's private secretary; he was already Member of Parliament for Woodstock (the family seat), and the four years they lived in Ireland served to whet his political appetite and aspirations. Both Randolph and Jennie hunted a great deal, and among Winston's earliest memories of his mother (seen below left, holding him) was of her in her riding habit . . . 'fitting like a skin and often beautifully spotted with mud'.

4

Winston Churchill was born on 30 November 1874 at his grandparents' historic home, Blenheim Palace. His birth was six weeks premature and precipitate – Lady Randolph gave birth downstairs. The illustration reproduced above is probably the earliest known photograph of Winston. Below, 'sailor-boy' Winston at five years old.

5

6

7

Randolph and Jennie's second and last child, Jack, was born in 1880. Although there were six years between them, Winston and Jack were devoted to each other throughout their lives. This photograph was taken in 1889 when Jack (left) was nine and Winston fourteen. Winston adored his beautiful mother, but, like many Edwardian parents, she and his father were distant deities. The guardian and confidante of Winston's and Jack's childhood days was their nurse – Mrs Everest (left). To the end of his life Winston was to recall 'Woom' (as he nicknamed her) with tenderness and gratitude.

10

Winston must often have seen his mother dressed for a ball: 'My mother always seemed
to me a fairy princess: a radiant being possessed of limitless
riches and power . . .' Jennie was a brilliant figure in London society, but she never failed
to play her part as the wife of a public figure and rapidly rising
politician, whether electioneering for her husband or, as we see in the picture below,
taking part in popular local events – in this case leading a tricycle rally.

12

13

'Here, Sir!' Winston at 'Bill' (roll call) at Harrow School. He went to Harrow in 1888, when he was nearly fourteen, and remained there for the next four years. His schooldays were not the happiest of his life: yet the magic of Harrow songs was to remain with him always. Winston showed promise only in the subjects he liked – history and English. His prodigious memory was already in training, and he won a prize for reciting Macaulay's *Lays of Ancient Rome*. Although he disliked conventional team games he was proficient at fencing, and won a silver medal in a competition. Lord and Lady Randolph rarely visited their schoolboy son, and Winston felt this keenly, often begging them, in his letters home, to come to Harrow; but they were bound up in the whirl of their political and social life. Jennie was a good and breezy correspondent, but his father's letters, for the most part critical and snubbing, strike a chilling note. Winston longed for his father's approval but Lord Randolph deemed him fit only for an army career. After a spell at a 'crammer', Winston passed into Sandhurst.

Lord Randolph became Secretary of State for India in 1885, and Chancellor of the Exchequer the following year; but he only held this office for six months, because he suddenly tendered his resignation in protest against certain proposals for Budget expenditure on the armed forces.

He made a fatal miscalculation – the Prime Minister (Lord Salisbury) accepted his resignation without demur. Lord Randolph was never to hold office again. Although remaining active in politics, his health soon began to decline – he had contracted syphilis. The last years of this brilliant but unstable man's life were increasingly marked by the progress of the fell (and, in those days, incurable) disease.

In the summer of 1894 Lord and Lady Randolph set out on a world tour. Randolph was so ill that he had to be accompanied by doctors. It must have been a melancholy journey. Randolph and Jennie are seen here in Japan. (The man in the right-hand rickshaw is a doctor.) The tour had to be curtailed because of Lord Randolph's rapidly declining health: they arrived home at Christmas time. On 24 January 1895 Randolph Spencer Churchill died. He was forty-six. This photograph of Jennie with her two sons (right) was taken soon after her husband's death. Winston – now the head of the family – has taken his mother's arm almost protectively. Although Jennie was always to use her (not inconsiderable) influence to help her son in his career, she burdened both Winston and Jack with her financial extravagance.

16

Winston had passed out of Sandhurst shortly before his father's death, and in February 1895
he was gazetted a second lieutenant. He joined the
4th Hussars, a cavalry regiment, then stationed at Aldershot.

17

The four years of Winston's service as a regular soldier were characterized by his constant (and successful) efforts to see action. During his first leave he nipped off to Cuba with a brother officer to take part in the campaign the Spaniards were conducting in Cuba against a guerrilla uprising. Winston heard bullets first whistle in anger in 1895 on his twenty-first birthday.

The following September the 4th Hussars sailed for India: they were quartered at Bangalore. Here Winston learned to play polo. The photograph below shows Winston with some of the regimental polo ponies and Indian syces (grooms) at Bangalore.

During the long hours of the daily siesta, Winston applied himself to a self-made programme of education. The young subaltern soaked his mind and fired his imagination with Gibbon, Macaulay and Plato. Volumes of the *Annual Register* fed his growing interest in politics.

In 1897 the Malakand Field Force was engaged upon reprisals against the nomadic tribes of the Indian North-west Frontier: Winston was granted extended leave from his regiment and, although not able to take part in the campaign in a military capacity (officially), the commanding general allowed him to be present as a newspaper correspondent. His letters from the field of action were published by the *Calcutta Pioneer* and in London by the *Daily Telegraph*. He earned a campaign medal and a Mention in Despatches before he was recalled to his own regiment. In the following months Winston wrote his first book, *The Story of the Malakand Field Force*, which was published in the spring of 1898. That same year he wrote and published his one and only novel, *Savrola*.

Meanwhile, Kitchener's army was preparing to avenge the death of General Gordon. Winston was accepted as an emergency replacement in the 21st Lancers, and it was with this regiment that he took part in the last great cavalry charge of history at the Battle of Omdurman on 2 September 1898 (above). Once more he reported on the campaign; this time his letters were published in the *Morning Post*. Back with his own regiment once again, he started another book based on his reports – *The River War*. As well as writing and soldiering, he was in the winning team in the All-India Inter-Regimental Polo Tournament.

19

20

21

22

23

At home in England during 1899, Winston earned his political spurs by contesting a by-election at Oldham in Lancashire as a Conservative. He was narrowly defeated by the Liberal candidate. But already action and adventure were calling again: by the early autumn of 1899 war between Britain and the Boer Republics was imminent. Winston arranged to go to South Africa as the correspondent for the *Morning Post*. Once arrived in Cape Town, he obtained a commission in a yeomanry regiment – the Lancashire Hussars (above). Once more he assumed the role of soldier-cum-war correspondent. There now occurred a series of events which were to take the form of an epic adventure story, and turn Winston into a popular hero. Seeking the scene of lively action Winston went to the Natal front and found the British troops at Estcourt. On 15 November 1899 he went on an armoured train which was making a reconnaissance into Boer-held territory, under the command of Captain Aylmer Haldane. The train was ambushed and derailed by Boers. During the ensuing skirmish under fierce fire, Winston took a prominent and gallant part – chiefly in organizing the clearing of part of the line so that the engine and tender, loaded with fifty or sixty men (some of them wounded), could get away, back along the line. Winston rejoined Captain Haldane and the remaining men, and they were all taken prisoner. They were taken to a prison camp in Pretoria (Winston can be seen on the right in the photograph above right). Winston found every day of imprisonment

intolerable. On 12 December he and Captain Haldane and a sergeant-major made a bid for freedom over the prison wall: in the event, only Winston succeeded in getting away. He waited in vain for the others, and then headed eastwards towards the Portuguese-Mozambique frontier on foot and by jumping trains. A reward of £25 was offered for his capture – dead or alive. Lost and exhausted, he eventually sought help at a mine, where by great good fortune the colliery manager, John Howard, was British-born (but a naturalized Transvaal citizen). He hid Winston down the mine, and after a few days sent him on his way in a freight train. Three days later Winston arrived safely in Lourenço Marques (now Maputo). By the time he arrived in Durban (left) his exploits had rung round the world, and he was accorded a hero's welcome. After these adventures Winston continued in his military-journalistic role, but now joined the South Africa Light Horse, also obtaining a commission for his brother Jack. The family group was completed by Lady Randolph's arrival in the hospital ship *Maine*, which had been purchased and equipped by an Anglo-American group. Jennie was the Executive Committee's representative on board. One of the first patients turned out to be Jack, who had been slightly wounded in a skirmish. The photograph shows Jennie with Jack on board the *Maine*.

24   25

In the summer of 1900 Lady Randolph Churchill married Mr George Cornwallis-West: she was forty-six, he was twenty years younger – the same age as Winston! They had met two years before, and it had been love at first sight. Their families and friends counselled them against marrying. George's family boycotted the wedding which took place in London on 28 July 1900. But Jennie's family (including the Marlboroughs) turned up in force, whatever their private reservations may have been.
September 1900 brought a General Election, and Winston once more contested Oldham. His mother, now Mrs Cornwallis-West, campaigned as enthusiastically for her son as she had done in years gone by for her husband. This time Winston was victorious at the polls. He made his maiden speech in February 1901 to a crowded House. With the briefest of intervals he was to be a Member of Parliament for over half a century.

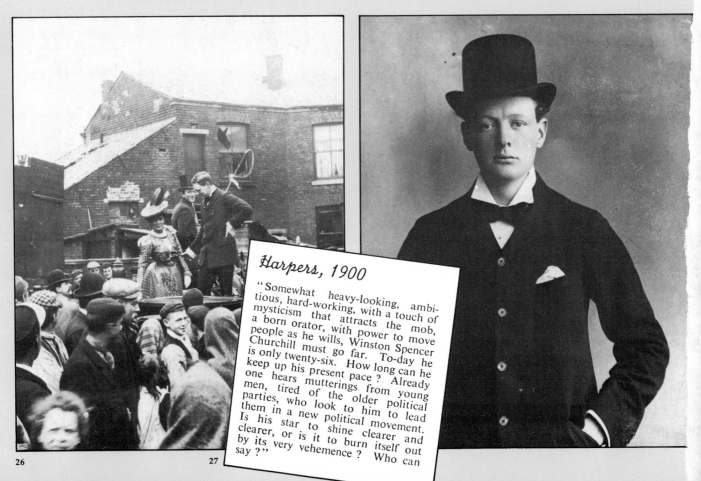

26   27

Harpers, 1900

"Somewhat heavy-looking, ambitious, hard-working, with a touch of mysticism that attracts the mob, a born orator, with power to move people as he wills, Winston Spencer Churchill must go far. To-day he is only twenty-six. How long can he keep up his present pace? Already one hears mutterings from young men, tired of the older political parties, who look to him to lead them in a new political movement. Is his star to shine clearer and clearer, or is it to burn itself out by its very vehemence? Who can say?"

29 30

The Duke of Marlborough or 'Sunny' (as he was usually known) was Winston's first cousin; he was a few years older, but, although their natures were very dissimilar, they were lifelong friends. Even after Winston became a Liberal and made fiery speeches about ducal privileges, and initiated and supported legislation which was anathema to his cousin, Sunny continued his friendship – although there were a few (soon forgotten) acerbities. In 1895 the duke had married the beautiful Miss Consuelo Vanderbilt of New York. It was a *mariage de convenance*, and Consuelo came to the altar in tears, having been literally forced into the marriage by her mother. Despite the incompatibility of their natures they remained together for eleven years: Consuelo bore her husband two sons, and presided with grace, intelligence and charm over Blenheim and the glittering social world into which she had so reluctantly married.

33

32

Here are some family snapshots taken in 1902–3 at Blenheim where Winston and Jack were frequent guests. The photograph on the left shows Jack with Consuelo and his mother, and that on the right Winston with Consuelo. The photograph in the centre shows Winston with Ethel Barrymore. At one time Winston became deeply enamoured of this famous actress, and proposed marriage to her. She declined. Many years later Miss Barrymore was to confirm this, adding that she had been much attracted by the young Winston Churchill, but had felt that the world of politics, which was his life, was not for her.

Although Winston had entered Parliament as a Conservative Unionist, he soon began to find himself at variance with his party. In 1903 Joseph Chamberlain proclaimed his belief in Protection and Tariff Reform, and a drift in opinion towards these views became evident in the Conservative Party.

But Winston was against Protection – and had already declared himself as a Free Trader to his constituents. He now began to find himself strongly out of sympathy with the mood and views of the Conservative Party. In December 1903, after Winston had sent a letter of support to a Liberal candidate at a by-election, the Conservative Whip was withdrawn from him. The following May Winston crossed the floor of the House to sit on the Liberal benches.

Winston's change of allegiance made him, in the eyes of many people, a renegade both from his party and his class. He found the great Tory houses closed to him. This was no great deprivation, for social activity for its own sake was neither then nor later to be of importance to him and Winston was always to maintain personal friendships across the lines of party politics.

However, at Crewe House, the London home of Lord Crewe – a prominent figure in the Liberal Party – Winston was a welcome guest; and it was at a ball at Crewe House during the summer season of 1904 that he first beheld and made the acquaintance of the beautiful Clementine Hozier. Winston saw her across the crowded room, and – deeply struck by her loveliness – asked his mother, who had accompanied him to the ball, to effect an introduction. But Winston, instead of engaging her in conversation or asking her to dance, simply stood rooted to the spot and stared at her! Much embarrassed, Clementine made a sign to a friend standing near-by, who rescued her by taking her off to dance.

Their paths were not to cross again for four years.

In December 1905, the Liberal leader, Sir Henry Campbell-Bannerman, formed a government in which Winston Churchill was given his first ministerial office – that of Under-Secretary of State for the Colonies. In the subsequent General Election (January – February 1906), which saw a 'landslide' Liberal victory, Winston won in North-West Manchester. In the Autumn of 1907, Churchill set out on an official journey to Africa. Pausing in Venice, he found his cousin Sunny Marlborough, somewhat disconsolate, he and Consuelo having recently separated. This snapshot of Winston in Venice was taken by Miss Gladys Deacon, a celebrated American beauty, and a brilliant figure in European society. Many years later she and Sunny Marlborough married each other. *My African Journey* (published 1908) was the literary fruit of Winston's journey.

37

38

39

Here is Winston very much 'on the job' at Malta on his way out to Africa. On Winston's right is Eddie Marsh, who came to Winston as his private secretary in 1905 and who was to serve him in all his offices until 1929. He became a lifelong friend and companion. He was a man of the highest intellectual accomplishment translating La Fontaine's *Fables* and the *Odes* of Horace. He was also a patron of the arts.

Clementine's early life

40

Clementine Hozier was a granddaughter of the 10th Earl of Airlie: Ogilvy is the family name, and its story stretches far back into Scottish history. Clementine's parents separated when she was nearly six, and thereafter, the four children, Kitty, Clementine, and the twins Bill and Nellie, were to live with their mother, Lady Blanche Hozier. After the breakdown of her marriage, Lady Blanche was very badly off financially; and partly because of this, and partly due to her own vagrant nature, she and her children led a somewhat nomadic existence. As was usual for children of their class, the girls were mostly educated at home by governesses. Kitty was (without disguise) her mother's favourite: nevertheless Clementine loved her elder sister devotedly – sheltering behind her more buoyant and dominating personality. When Kitty died in her seventeenth year, Clementine was grief-struck and bereft. Their father, Sir Henry Hozier, either completely ignored his wife and children, or made sudden descents, which alarmed and unsettled them – especially the more nervous Clementine. Yet, as she grew older, she had a great desire to know her father better: but this was not to be, and he died in 1907, a year before she married. Throughout her childhood and adolescence Clementine suffered much unhappiness because of her mother's uneven affections and hasty temperament; and her own lifelong reserve and shyness in personal relationships stem from these difficult years, and they belied a nature which was spontaneous, sensitive and passionate.

Lady Blanche Ogilvy (1852–1925) was beautiful, wayward and fascinating to men. She was
twenty-six when she married Henry Hozier. For five years they had no children,
and then in 1883 Kitty was born, followed by Clementine in 1885, and Bill and Nellie –
the twins – in 1888. The marriage was not a happy one, and after several stormy
upheavals, Blanche and Henry Hozier separated for ever in 1891, when Clementine was
nearly six. Colonel Sir Henry Montague Hozier KCB (1838–1907) had a brilliant mind
and a strange, and at times somewhat violent, character. Entering upon a military career,
he held various important staff posts, and wrote several historical books and treatises.
Leaving the army aged thirty-six, he was appointed Secretary to Lloyds of London,
the great insurance underwriters, which post he held for thirty-two years with outstanding
success and distinction. His first marriage ended in divorce, and shortly afterwards,
in 1878, he married Lady Blanche Henrietta Ogilvy, the elder daughter of the Earl and
Countess of Airlie. At forty he was fourteen years older than his bride.

43

44

Kitty and Clementine with their Swiss governess Mlle Elise Aeschimann, photographed outside The Netherton, the Hoziers' small house in Scotland. Mlle Elise quickly spotted that Kitty was her mother's favourite, and so she was particularly protective and tender to Clementine, who remembered her governess's kindness all her life, and kept in touch with her until she died. Bill and Nellie, the twins, were about five when this photograph was taken.

45

Kitty (left) and Clementine. The children's lives were divided between their parents' London house in Grosvenor Street, and here at The Netherton, which was in the same neighbourhood as Airlie Castle, where their grandmother lived, and Cortachy Castle, the home of their uncle and aunt, the Earl and Countess of Airlie, and their Ogilvy cousins.

After Blanche and Henry Hozier parted The Netherton was abandoned, and the children
used to spend a great part of their summer holidays staying with their grandmother
at Airlie Castle – a small castle, perched on a precipitous rock above a gorge through which
flows the river Isla. Blanche, Countess of Airlie was a clever, cultivated woman of
redoubtable character. Her grandchildren held her in awe, and revered rather than
loved her. This photograph of Lady Airlie was taken in about 1904.

48

With only two years between them, Clementine and Kitty were constant companions and
the closest of friends. Their personalities, however, were very
different: Kitty was ever the leader – pretty, saucy and buoyant, she was also
her mother's declared favourite. Clementine as a small child was not
pretty, and tended to be timid and tearful. She was in every way outshone by Kitty,
behind whose more confident personality she was only too glad to hide.
Their mother's open favouritism never made the least rift between the sisters.

49

Although the children were brought up by their mother, their father Henry Hozier, even *in absentia*, was to be a dominating feature in their lives, and his sudden reappearances were a cause for anxiety and alarm, especially to the somewhat fearful Clementine. After she separated from her husband, Blanche Hozier and her children led a restless life between rented houses and furnished lodgings. The children's education, however, was never neglected, and they always had either a French or German governess. In 1899 Blanche Hozier, with typical suddenness, moved from Seaford to Dieppe, just across the Channel. There she rented a house and sent Kitty (seen above; sixteen), Clementine (fourteen) and Nellie (eleven) to a nearby convent school. Bill was now at a preparatory school in England. A short while before her seventeenth birthday, Kitty (above) became ill with typhoid fever and died. The picture below shows her on her deathbed.

Kitty Ogilvy Hozier. April 18ᵗʰ 1883. March 5ᵗʰ 1900.

50

After the shock and anguish of Kitty's death Blanche Hozier packed up and returned to England, settling for the next four years or so in Berkhamsted in Hertfordshire, choosing this place because of the excellent High Schools in the town, to which all three children – Clementine, Nellie and Bill – now went.
Kitty's death marked a watershed in Clementine's life. From then on she was to be a lonely figure in the family group between her grief-stricken mother and the twins.

Clementine Ogilvy Hozier. August. 1901.

51

Clementine started now to become the woman she was to be: her affectionate – even passionate – nature was concealed behind a certain reserve and formality; she learned to keep her own counsel, and to hide her inmost feelings. The sparkling side of her nature found room for expression at school, and her years at Berkhamsted High School were happy ones; she relished the competition after the limitations of governess education, and she relished the team games. This photograph shows Clementine in her seventeenth year. The classical beauty shines through the austere simplicity of the schoolgirl.

Clementine was introduced into the London world when she was eighteen by a great aunt, Lady St Helier. Her own mother could not undertake this then indispensable task herself through a combination of lack of money and the fact of the separation from her husband – a serious social inconvenience in those days. Lady St Helier took Clementine about, and gave her her first ball gown; very soon her beauty, liveliness and charm earned Clementine both invitations and admirers.

Blanche Hozier and her family moved back now into London, and lived at 51 Abingdon Villas, behind Kensington High Street. To earn some much needed pin-money, Clementine, whose French was excellent, started giving French lessons. She also worked for some time for a cousin who had a dressmaking business.

52

53

54

55

When she was eighteen, Clementine had met the Hon. Sidney Peel, a man of brilliance and distinction, some fifteen years older than herself. He was to become her most devoted and tenacious admirer. He loved her deeply, and she very nearly persuaded herself that she loved him, for she was twice secretly engaged to him. Over thirty years later she read of his death in *The Times* while she was travelling in the West Indies. She was to write to Winston: 'Time stood still, fell away, and I lived again those four years during which I saw him nearly every day – He was good to me and made my difficult rather arid life interesting – But I couldn't care for him & I was not kind or even very grateful – And then my Darling you came and in that moment I knew the difference . . .'

Clementine (standing on left) was bridesmaid to her cousin
and lifelong friend the Hon. Sylvia Stanley when she married
Colonel Anthony Henley in April 1906. She was now just
twenty-one. Sylvia's sisters, Venetia and Blanche, are seated left
and right. Venetia later married Edwin Montagu, and was
the great friend and confidante of Mr Asquith
when he was Prime Minister.

Horatia Seymour was a few years older than Clementine. She
was both brilliant and beautiful. She befriended
Clementine when she first started going to parties and staying
away in country houses where they were often fellow guests.
They had much in common – including being badly off.
Their friendship was to last a lifetime. Although she had many
admirers, Horatia Seymour never married.

Engagement and marriage

August 15, 1908.

ENGAGEMENT OF MR. CHURCHILL.

Marriage Arranged with Miss Clementine Hozier.

YOUNGEST MINISTER.

Romantic Betrothal to Daughter of Distinguished Soldier.

EARL OF AIRLIE'S COUSIN

58

In the spring of 1908, Winston and Clementine met once more – it was four years since their first meeting at the Crewe House ball, which had been marred by Winston's social clumsiness. Now they were fellow guests of Lady St Helier (the benevolent relation who had taken Clementine under her wing). It was, in fact, a chance meeting, for Clementine had been invited at the last moment by her great aunt, to fill a gap at her table. Mr Winston Churchill M.P., and Under-Secretary for the Colonies, arriving late for dinner (punctuality was never to be among his virtues), found that he was seated next to Miss Clementine Hozier, the girl whose looks he had already so much admired: and now, he was not only once more smitten by her beauty, but he also found her charming, vivacious, and intelligent. And *this* time he did not muff his chances! Practically ignoring the lady on his other side, Winston concentrated on Clementine, who was swept away by his brilliance and captivating charm. A few weeks later, his mother Jennie Cornwallis-West invited Lady Blanche Hozier and Clementine to stay for the weekend at her country house, Salisbury Hall, near St Albans. And it was during this weekend, on 12 April, that Mr Asquith (who had just become Prime Minister) announced his Government, in which Winston Churchill (aged thirty-three) entered the Cabinet as President of the Board of Trade. Truly his star –both in love and politics – was in the ascendant!

The betrothed couple. This photograph was taken by Margaret Smith (Mrs F.E. Smith)
at the time of their engagement.

60

61

For the month following the engagement their courtship had to be conducted through the post, for Clementine was on the eve of a long-planned journey to the Continent with her mother, and Winston (as was customary then) had, on becoming a senior minister, to seek re-election. He therefore had to fight a by-election in North-west Manchester. On this occasion he was defeated – but a short while later he was elected at Dundee, a seat he was to hold for fourteen years.

62

On 4 August 1908, Jack Churchill married Lady Gwendeline Bertie (daughter of the Earl of Abingdon). Always called 'Goonie', she and Clementine, as sisters-in-law, were to become the closest of friends and confidantes.

Winston asked his cousin Sunny Marlborough to invite Clementine to Blenheim Palace: he had determined to ask her to marry him – and where better than at Blenheim? It was a place which had so many associations, not only with the historical glory of England and his great ancestor, John, Duke of Marlborough. Blenheim after all was where he himself had seen the light of day, and to which, throughout his life, ties of kinship, affection and friendship would always draw him.

The Duke, to whom Winston had confided his intentions, gladly invited Clementine. Also in the house-party, somewhat hastily assembled, were Jennie Cornwallis-West and Mr and Mrs F. E. Smith (F.E. was one of Winston's greatest friends).

Winston took Clementine for a walk in the grounds – they were overtaken by a rainstorm, and took refuge in the little Temple of Diana which looks out over the great lake: here Winston proposed to her, and she accepted him.

Here is the page from the Blenheim Visitors' Book signed by the guests at the engagement house-party. Winston and Clementine next signed the book (at the bottom of the same page) after spending the first few days of their honeymoon at Blenheim.

Clementine Hozier: an engagement picture.

66

Both Winston and Jack were officers in the Oxfordshire Yeomanry, whose summer camps were often held in the park at Blenheim. While their menfolk 'played at soldiers' – in only a few years it would become a grim reality – many of their ladies stayed at the Palace with the Duke and his family; so the Yeomanry camps were an enjoyable feature of the summer season. Here is a group photograph taken in the short period between Jack and Goonie's wedding in early August, and that of Winston and Clementine in September. Some faces and names of interest to us are:

Standing at the back: Fourth from left, Jack Churchill, and extreme right at the end of that row, Col. Gordon Wilson (married to Sarah, one of Sunny Marlborough's sisters).

Second row: Third from left, Goonie Churchill, Jack's newly-wed wife. Next to her, right, Lady Norah Spencer-Churchill (another of the Duke's sisters). The florid-looking gentleman in the bowler hat is the Marquis de Soveral, for many years the Portuguese Ambassador in London, and a frequent figure in Edwardian society.

Third row seated: Left, Lady Sarah Wilson (another sister, we have noted her husband above), next to the Duke of Wellington. Sitting in the middle between two dominating ladies (the one to the left being the Duchess of Wellington), is the young King of Portugal, who was staying at Blenheim at the time. One away from the King to the right is another of the Duke's sisters, Lady Lilian Grenfell; and one from the end of that row, Miss Clementine Hozier, soon to become Mrs Winston Churchill.

Front row: Fifth from left is Sunny, the Duke of Marlborough. And third from right, Winston Churchill.

67

The marriage was arranged for 12 September, thus enabling the bridegroom to be back at his ministerial desk after the honeymoon by the time Parliament reassembled: this left only the minimum time to prepare for the event, and Clementine was swept away on a tidal wave of wedding arrangements. A somewhat exhausted bride wrote to Winston: 'Thinking about you has been the only pleasant thing today. I have tried on so many garments (all of which I am told are indispensable) . . .' The wedding was to take place at St Margaret's, Westminster (the parish church of the House of Commons).

Benevolent Lady St Helier (Clementine's great aunt) lent her house in Portland Place for the reception; and before travelling on the Continent, the first few days of the honeymoon would be passed at Blenheim Palace. The public found this match most romantic and pleasing; and, in the weeks before the wedding, accounts of the bride's shopping expeditions and other details were recorded, and the events of the great day itself monopolized large portions of newsprint. This picture shows sketches of the bride's dress, and a bridesmaid's dress and hat. The bridesmaids (see opposite) were: Clementine's sister Nellie; Madeleine Whyte and Venetia Stanley, her cousins; Horatia Seymour, her closest friend; and Clare Frewen, Winston's cousin. Clementine was given away by her brother Bill. The wedding was a brilliant affair for the political and social world: St Margaret's overflowed with guests, and there were large crowds to cheer the happy pair.

MR. WINSTON CHURCHILL'S BRIDE AND HER BRIDESMAIDS.

Central Photograph by Paterson, Inverness.

FIEL·PERO·DESDICHADO

MISS HORATIA SEYMOUR

MISS MADELEINE WHYTE

THE HON. VENETIA STANLEY

MISS CLARE FREWEN

MISS NELLIE HOZIER

THE DAILY GRAPHIC
ONE PENNY

No. 5852.—Vol. LXXV.

LONDON: MONDAY, SEPTEMBER 14, 1908.

Registered as a Newspaper.

THE MARRIAGE OF A CABINET MINISTER.

THE BRIDESMAIDS.

MR. CHURCHILL AND HIS BRIDE PASSING DOWN THE NAVE AFTER THE MARRIAGE CEREMONY.

THE BRIDEGROOM ARRIVES AT THE CHURCH.
("Daily Graphic" Photograph.)

THE CHURCHILL-HOZIER WEDDING AT ST. MARGARET'S, WESTMINSTER, ON SATURDAY AFTERNOON.   (See page 3.)

The Daily Mirror

THE MORNING JOURNAL WITH THE SECOND LARGEST NET SALE.

No. 1,522.   Registered at the G. P. O. as a Newspaper.   MONDAY, SEPTEMBER 14, 1908.   One Halfpenny.

MR. WINSTON CHURCHILL MARRIED TO MISS CLEMENTINE HOZIER AT ST. MARGARET'S, WESTMINSTER.

The most popular and interesting wedding of the year took place on Saturday at St. Margaret's, Westminster, when Mr. Winston Churchill, President of the Board of Trade, married Miss Clementine Hozier, daughter of Lady Blanche Hozier and the late Colonel Sir Henry Hozier, in the presence of over a thousand guests, many of them distinguished in politics, science, art, and literature. An enormous crowd assembled in Parliament-square to see the arrival and departure of the bride and bridegroom. (1) Miss Hozier arrives with her brother, Sub-Lieutenant Hozier, R.N. (2) Mr. and Mrs. Churchill leaving the church. (3) Miss Nellie Hozier, chief bridesmaid, with her brother. (4) The other four bridesmaids—(A) Miss Madeleine Whyte, (B) Miss Claire Frewen, (C) the Hon. Venetia Stanley, (D) Miss Horatia Seymour.

Together: the early years

71

When they married, Winston swept Clementine into the whirl and excitement of the political world which he inhabited. Now was the floodtide of the reforming Liberal government which had come overwhelmingly to power in 1906. Winston's whole life was politics, and although the circumstances and pace of Clementine's life hitherto had been vastly different – yet her qualities of mind and temperament made her well able to swim in the midstream of the fascinating world in which she now found herself. To the interest of politics were added the problems of housekeeping on a relatively small income, for a husband of a gregarious and extravagant nature, who, as someone remarked, 'was easily satisfied with the very best'! Soon, too, came the fulfilments and ties of motherhood: Clementine relished her babies, and Winston was a particularly tender and solicitous father. But, as time went on, the competition between the children's claims and Winston's life became more marked: there was never any doubt, however, as to who would be the winner of this contest – Winston, both now and forever, would be Clementine's first priority – before children, friends, and her own interests. The pattern for their half century together seems to have been set in this early period: the tension of political life; the participation in world-shaking events; the hopes and disappointments; the triumphs, and the catastrophic 'downs'. And through·all, their mutual, tenderly expressed love for each other, which was to endure unfaltering, to the end.

72

This charming photograph of Winston and Clementine in the early years of their marriage (it was taken on manoeuvres at Aldershot in 1910) seems to express a joyful, confident setting out together.

73

74

Shortly after returning from their honeymoon Winston took his bride to Scotland to introduce her to
his constituents in Dundee. On the way they visited Clementine's grandmother, Blanche,
Countess of Airlie. This photograph was taken in October 1908 in the garden at Airlie Castle.
After their marriage, they first lived in Winston's small bachelor house in Bolton Street, Mayfair.
But with the expectation of their first child something larger was necessary,
and in early May 1909 they moved into their first real home, No. 33 Eccleston Square (above).
Below, Clementine is pictured in the throes of moving house assisted by a friend.

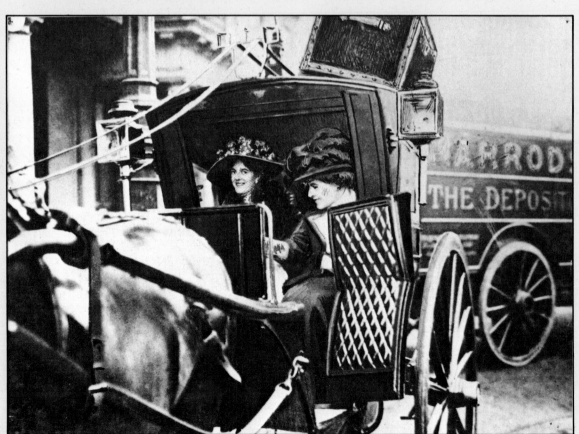

75

Winston and Clementine's first child, Diana, was born at 33 Eccleston Square on 11 July 1909.

Whenever they were separated, even for a few days, Winston and Clementine wrote to each other. An absence as short as forty-eight hours sometimes found two or three letters flying between them.

These early days of their marriage saw the beginning of that long dialogue on paper which was to last over half a century, and which bears such vivid and moving testimony to their relationship. Early on they assumed 'pet' names: Winston was the 'Pug' and Clementine 'Clemmie', or 'the Cat' (usually spelt 'Kat'); and they signed their letters or decorated their signatures with charming little drawings. 'I must have lessons in Kat-drawing,' Clementine wrote in one of her letters, 'as your pugs are so much better than my Kats.'

Presently Winston changed from 'Pug' to 'Pig' (perhaps he found pigs easier to draw); and throughout their long correspondence pigs appear in various attitudes and moods.

Clementine's 'Kats' may have been less daring artistically, but they were full of character and most expressive of her feelings.

Here are some examples of their Pug–Pig–Kat devices.

In September 1909 Winston attended the German army manoeuvres
at the personal invitation of Kaiser Wilhelm II. He was deeply impressed by the display
of military might which unrolled before him. He wrote to Clementine: 'This army is a terrible
engine . . . It is in number as the sands of the sea . . . Much as war attracts me
& fascinates my mind with its tremendous situations – I feel more deeply every year – & can
measure the feeling here in the midst
of arms – what vile and wicked folly and barbarism it all is.'

In January/February 1910 there took place the first of two General Elections which were destined to be held within twelve months: they were precipitated by the violent constitutional struggle between the Lords and Commons touched off by Lloyd George's famous (or to some, infamous) 'People's Budget' which he had introduced in the spring of 1909. Passed by the House of Commons in early November, it was thrown out by the House of Lords a few weeks later. Asquith thereupon called for a dissolution of Parliament and went to the country. Although the Liberals won, they lost their absolute majority, and had to depend upon the support of Irish Nationalist M.P.s. In the reconstruction of the government in February 1910, the Prime Minister moved Churchill from the Board of Trade to the Home Office. The summer of 1910 saw widespread industrial unrest. After a second General Election in December, the parliamentary picture was virtually unchanged. In the New Year of 1911 Asquith introduced the Parliament Bill, designed to curb the powers of the House of Lords. It was passed through both Houses, after unparalleled scenes of violence and hysteria, in August that year.

81

During his time as President of the Board of Trade, Churchill had been responsible for promoting many reforming measures chiefly concerned with hours and conditions of labour. Among the most important schemes he inaugurated was the setting up of Labour Exchanges throughout the country as a means of alleviating unemployment. Among his advisers was Mr (later Sir) William Beveridge, whose historic report in 1942 laid the foundations of the Welfare State: he was appointed the first Director of Labour Exchanges. The picture above shows the Prime Minister, Mr Asquith, with Winston and Clementine during a tour they made of newly opened Labour Exchanges in the London area in February 1910.

82

This photograph shows Winston accompanying Mr and Mrs Lloyd George to the House of Commons on Budget Day in April 1910. The 'People's Budget' – rejected by the House of Lords in the previous November – now passed through both Houses.

Hunting . . . shooting . . . fishing . . . a programme of life for many in the
world to which Winston belonged by birth, were spasmodic distractions
for him. Hunting and polo he enjoyed most of all. But a good day's
shooting was also a pleasure and, considering how rarely he did it, he was a
remarkably good shot. Here he is shooting in December 1910 at
Warter Priory in Yorkshire, at that time the home of the Nunburnholme
family. Winston had written to Clementine (kept at home
in London with a bad cold): 'A nice party – puissant, presentable, radical
in preponderance – a rare combination, I wish you were here . . .
Tomorrow pheasants in thousands – the vy best wot ever was seen. Tonight
Poker – I lost a little – but the play was low. On the whole
survey, how much more power and great business are to me, than this
kind of thing, pleasant tho it seems by contrast to our
humble modes of entertainment!' Clementine wrote back indulgently:
'Dearest, you work so hard and have so little fun in your life.
I wish you had more of this sort of thing . . .'

Winston always took his duties as a reservist very seriously and regularly
attended the annual summer camps of the Queen's Own Oxfordshire
Yeomanry. Here he is map-reading at
manoeuvres which were held on Salisbury Plain in 1910.

85

In January 1911 there occurred an incident which became known as 'The Battle of Sidney Street'.
Some anarchists had barricaded themselves into a house and engaged in a running
gun-battle with the police (a more uncommon event then than now!). Troops had to be called in,
and, as Home Secretary, Winston had to give the necessary permission. Needless to say
he could not resist the lure of action and excitement, and went to the scene himself.
In the picture he is seen on the extreme left of the group of police. His presence
in Sidney Street called down upon his head much criticism both from Press and Parliament:
and those who were apt to be critical of Winston
Churchill chalked this up as one more instance of rash and ill-judged conduct.

86

Winston with his mother,
Jennie Cornwallis-West, in 1911.

87

On 28 May 1911, Winston and Clementine's only
son was born at their home in Eccleston Square.
Here is a christening photograph. His godfathers were
Sir Edward Grey, the Foreign Secretary,
and Mr F. E. Smith, who
was to have a strong influence on Randolph
in his youth.

88

Winston and Clementine seen driving to the Coronation of King George V and Queen Mary in June 1911. Clementine was only able to attend as a result of the solicitude of the King himself. She was feeding Randolph, and could not, in normal circumstances, have attended so long a ceremony. But the King gave instructions that a carriage should be available immediately after the crowning, to whisk Clementine back to the ravenous Randolph.

89

After an exhausting and exciting summer, Clementine spent some weeks at Seaford with Diana (with whom she is seen here) and Randolph.

In October 1911, Mr Asquith, the Prime Minister, made some changes in his Cabinet. He moved Churchill from the Home Office to be First Lord of the Admiralty. This was the job Winston had for some time coveted – and the task for which he was supremely fitted. Here Clementine, proud and smiling, accompanies Winston on the occasion of the launch of the battleship HMS *Iron Duke*.

Churchill was always a favourite target for the Suffragettes, who since 1905 had mounted a campaign against politicians. Interruptions of meetings were commonplace, but personal physical attacks also became part of the Suffragettes' tactics. One had even tried to push Winston under a moving train. In 1913 threats were made to kidnap the children, and for a while police protection for them was deemed necessary. Here Nanny Higgs (right) sets out from Admiralty House (the official residence of the First Lord of the Admiralty where the Churchills now lived) with her nursery maid and the two prams, under the watchful eye of a detective.

Playing bears . . . Winston and Clementine with Randolph.

In 1912 Winston made his first flight in an aeroplane; thereafter he made many more flights, and in 1913 started to learn to fly himself. The Royal Naval Air Service was Winston's conception, and he watched over every detail of its development with the keenest interest. He had been swift to grasp the implications for the future of air power in terms of the country's defence and fighting strength. Fascinated by the development of the aeroplane, and filled with admiration for the brave men who were its pioneers (among whom the toll of life was very heavy), Winston wished to share in the adventure with all its dangers. During 1913, Winston completed many hours' flying instruction at various naval air stations. These activities, however, were the cause of deep anxiety to Clementine, and also to his friends, several of whom wrote to remonstrate with him and to endeavour to persuade him to abandon flying, which could in no way be described as part of his duty as First Lord of the Admiralty: but he was deaf to all appeals. In 1914, Clementine was again with child, and, after a letter from her in June which revealed to him the depth of her torment and anxiety, Winston agreed to give up flying, at least until after the birth of the baby. In telling her of his decision he wrote: 'So I give it up decidedly for many months & perhaps for ever. This is a gift – so stupidly am I made – wh costs me more than anything wh cd be bought with money. So I am vy glad to lay it at your feet, because I know that it will rejoice & relieve your heart . . .'

When Churchill went to the Admiralty in 1911, one of his first actions was to lure back from retirement as his special adviser the seventy-year-old Admiral of the Fleet Lord Fisher, whose brilliance in naval matters was acknowledged by all. But 'Jacky' Fisher was an eccentric and volcanic character, evoking mixed reactions within the service itself. Nevertheless, Churchill and Fisher worked well together, united in their desire to see Britain's fleet prepared against all eventualities. In October 1914, Lord Fisher succeeded Prince Louis of Battenberg as First Sea Lord. It was an appointment which was to prove disastrous in personal terms to Winston when the Dardanelles crisis broke in 1915. In this picture, however, we have the youthful First Lord of the Admiralty in jovial conversation with his friend and adviser – the veteran Admiral, Lord Fisher, in 1913.

94

This picture shows Winston in the cockpit: with his back turned to the camera is Captain Wildman-Lushington RM, with whom Winston had made many instructional flights. A few days after this photograph was taken, Captain Wildman-Lushington was killed while flying. In a letter to his fiancée, Miss Airlie Hynes, Winston wrote: 'To be killed instantly without pain or fear in the necessary service of the country when one is quite happy and life is fully of success & hope, cannot be reckoned the worst of fortune. But to some who are left behind the loss is terrible . . .' The wreath sent by Winston was composed of laurel leaves.

95

Clementine loved riding, although it had not come much into her life before she married;
but Winston encouraged her to have lessons, and whenever opportunity offered
they rode together – hiring good horses from livery stables. Clementine hunted several
times in 1912 and 1913, either staying at Blenheim, or with Winston's other cousins,
the Guests in Leicestershire. Clementine was generally energetic and athletic, greatly
enjoying not only riding but also tennis and golf. Here is Clementine taking
part in the Ladies' Parliamentary Golf Tournament at Ranelagh in 1913. Winston also
played golf occasionally – but polo was really his game.

96

97

During the best part of the summer of 1914, Clementine (who was expecting her third child in the autumn) and her sister-in-law Goonie installed themselves with their young broods and attendant nannies in two cottages by the sea at Overstrand, near Cromer. Clementine and her party inhabited Pear Tree Cottage, while Goonie and her family lived nearby in Beehive Cottage. Winston and Clementine (above) on the beach at Overstrand, and (right) Jack outside Beehive Cottage. The four children, Diana and Randolph, Johnnie and Peregrine, made a happy group. But in the background of this sunlit seaside scene, dark clouds were rolling up. Because of grave political events, Winston could only snatch a few Sundays away to join his family: but those days were happy and precious ones. After a day spent with them all, Winston wrote to Clementine: 'The kittens were vy dear & caressing. They get more lovable every day. Altogether Pear Tree is a vy happy, sunlit picture in my mind's eye . . .'

On 17–18 July 1914 a Grand Review of the Fleet took place: ships from all Britain's Fleets passed before King George V on board the Royal Yacht at Spithead. Churchill was to write later that it was '. . . incomparably the greatest assemblage of naval power ever witnessed in the history of the world'. Since his appointment as First Lord of the Admiralty in 1911, Winston's entire thought and energy had been concentrated on the building up of this tremendous navy. Later, in the shambles of the failure of the Dardanelles operation, when his own career seemed in ruins (some people thought forever), a colleague said to him: 'Whatever happens, they can't take that away from you – the Fleet was ready.' Moreover, it was not only ready – it was mobilized. After the Review the ships began dispersing to their own ports, and the reserve crews began demobilizing: by this time Austria had delivered her ultimatum, and Europe was trembling on the brink of war. Therefore Prince Louis of Battenberg (the First Sea Lord), fully supported by Churchill, gave orders to halt the dispersal of the Fleet.

So when the dread hour came, Britain's warships were at their stations.

101

Back in London, the Cabinet met often and sat long. Winston is here seen arriving by cab in Downing Street during the summer of 1914.
On Sunday 2 August 1914, at 1 a.m., Winston dashed off a letter to Clementine. On 3 August Germany invaded Belgium and declared war on France. Great Britain issued an ultimatum which expired at 11 p.m. on 4 August. Great Britain and Germany were at war.

2. 8. 14
1 am.

Cat ~ dear ~
It is all up. Germany
has quenched the last
hopes of peace by
declaring war on
Russia, a the declaration
against France is
momentarily expected.

102

Clementine, now well advanced in her pregnancy, very wisely stayed on at the seaside, much though she longed to be with Winston at the hub of events. Like every family in the land, they too had their anxieties. Jack Churchill went off to France with the Oxfordshire Yeomanry; Bill Hozier (left) was at sea, commanding HMS *Thorn*, a torpedo destroyer.
Clementine's sister Nellie (centre) joined a privately organized and financed nursing unit with which she went to Belgium. She and her companions were taken prisoner by the Germans during the confusion of the retreat after the Battle of Mons but they were repatriated two months later. Clementine's third child – a daughter – was born early on the morning of 7 October 1914 at Admiralty House. Four days before, Winston had suddenly dashed off to represent the Government at the siege of Antwerp. He arrived home on the 7th, to find a much relieved Clementine and a newly arrived red-headed daughter. They named her Sarah. This picture (above right) shows Sarah at about seven months with her mother.

Here is a grand line-up in 1915, at Admiralty House. Left to right: Winston, Diana, Clementine with Sarah on her lap, Randolph, Jennie Cornwallis-West, Goonie with Peregrine on her lap, Johnnie, Jack Churchill.

1915 saw the continuation of the grim slogging-match between the entrenched armies on the Western Front, to which the long casualty lists bore bitter witness. In this year also the Dardanelles operation was launched – and miserably failed. In the preceding months, Churchill had been the foremost protagonist of the plan to force the Dardanelles – arguing his case in the War Council and carrying his colleagues with him. It was in after years acknowledged to have been one of the few brilliant strategic concepts of the First World War, and had it succeeded, would have shortened its duration by months – if not years. Errors of judgement both on the spot and back in London, combined with ill-fortune, conspired to ruin the operation. At the height of the dramatic events which swiftly succeeded one another after the launch of the attack, Admiral of the Fleet Lord Fisher suddenly resigned on 15 May. His resignation, combined with bad news from other war fronts, touched off an already brewing political crisis. Asquith, in close consultation with Lloyd George, decided to form a Coalition Government: the Conservative leaders demanded, as their price for entering the new administration, the removal of Churchill from the Admiralty. In the new Coalition Government, Churchill was Chancellor of the Duchy of Lancaster
(an office with no executive power). Winston only accepted this humiliating demotion, because he was to remain in the Cabinet and War Council: feeling as he did such a deep responsibility for the Dardanelles operation, he desired above everything to see it through, and to do his utmost to retrieve the tragic situation. Many years later, looking back over their life, packed with dramatic events and political ups and downs, Clementine was to say that this was the darkest and most bitter hour for them both.

108

107

Right: I think this must be the earliest photograph of Winston painting. Clementine watches this new development approvingly: she was his best critic – although he was not always receptive to her advice. Far right: Grandmama Jennie, with Johnnie, Randolph and Diana at Hoe Farm (above).

109

Winston and Clementine made all haste to pack up and move out of Admiralty House. Their own house in Eccleston Square was let, but a relation lent them his London house while they made plans. For the summer months of 1915 they rented Hoe Farm, near Godalming in Surrey: here they installed the children (and Jack and Goonie's as well). It proved a haven for them for weekends and holidays, and it was also the place where Winston made a discovery which was to affect his whole life – he discovered painting!
Wandering round the garden brooding on his many worries, Winston found Goonie sketching: she encouraged him to try for himself. Fascinated, Winston borrowed Johnnie's paint-box – the Muse of Painting had come to his rescue! Winston henceforth had an occupation which was to be his joy and solace till very nearly the end of his life.

Relieved of a large house and the entertaining at Admiralty House, Clementine now sought some war work. She joined the new committee formed by the Young Men's Christian Association (Y.M.C.A.) to help in providing more adequate feeding arrangements for the munitions workers in the rapidly increasing number of factories, which were manufacturing arms day and night. She undertook the organization of canteens in the northern and north-eastern areas of London: which work she continued to do until the end of the war.

110

Here Clementine is addressing an audience when she opened the first Y.M.C.A. hut canteen for women munitions workers at Angel Road, Edmonton, in August 1915.
It was important that public morale should be kept high. The munitions factories provided large audiences. Winston is addressing munitions workers at Enfield Lock.

111

112

No. 41 Cromwell Road: Jack and Goonie Churchill's house, where the two brothers' families combined forces after Winston and Clementine moved out of Admiralty House in 1915. The two families lived together until the last year of the war.

113

Bereft of the great service department to which he had devoted his thought and energy for three years, and gnawed by the ever-increasing realization that his present position was one of responsibility without effective power – these months after leaving the Admiralty were a bleak period for Winston, and the thought of resignation was often in his mind. In November 1915, it was decided to reduce the size of the Dardanelles Committee of which he was a member: the reconstructed committee did not include him. This was the final breaking-point and on 11 November Winston Churchill resigned from the Government. A few days later he made a statement to the House of Commons, as is the right of ministers on resignation.
He then began his preparations to go out to France
to join his regiment, in which he held the rank of Major.
Winston left for France on 18 November 1915. This photograph was taken of him just after he had left the house, having made his farewells to his family. Clementine later wrote to tell him she had cut the picture out of the newspaper: . . . 'There was a thick fog & the figure is misty & dim & so I feel you receding into the fog & mud of Flanders & not coming back for so long . . .'

114

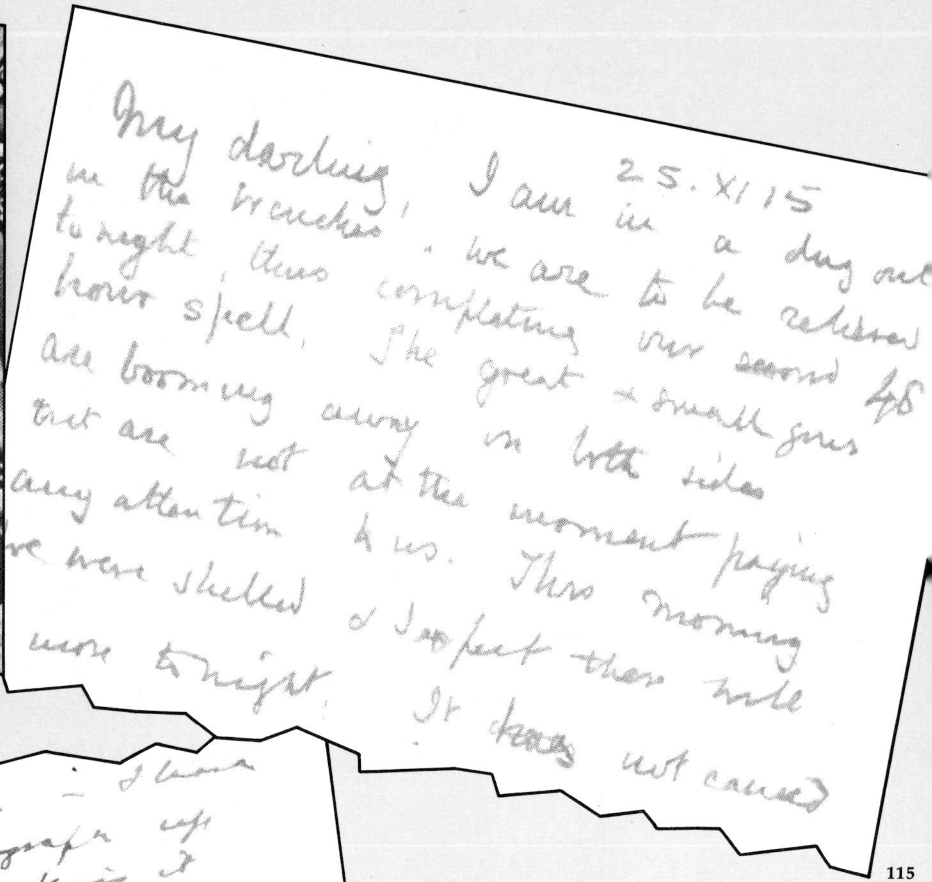

My darling, I am in a dug out in the trenches. We are to be relieved to night, thus completing our second 48 hour spell. The great & small guns are booming away on both sides but are not at the moment paying any attention to us. This morning we were shelled & I expect there will be more to night. It does not cause

115

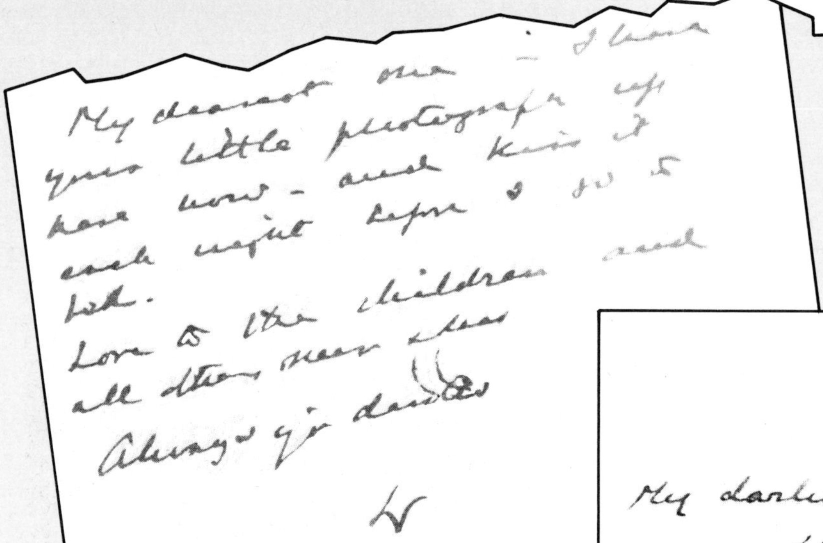

My dearest one — I have your little photograph up here now — and kiss it each night before I go to bed.

Love to the children and all others near & dear

Always yr devoted

W

116

When Winston Churchill went out to France in November 1915 he was to serve in front-line regiments for six bitter winter months before returning home. During this time he and Clementine wrote almost every day to one another, and their letters are not only of historic interest but also deeply moving. This photograph was taken while Churchill was commanding the 6th Battalion Royal Scots Fusiliers. He is wearing a glengarry, but, although extremely proud to be serving with a Scots regiment, he thought the Scots 'bonnet' did not really suit him: so he resumed the *poilu*'s helmet, which had been presented to him while on a visit to a French regiment, and which he is wearing in the picture opposite.

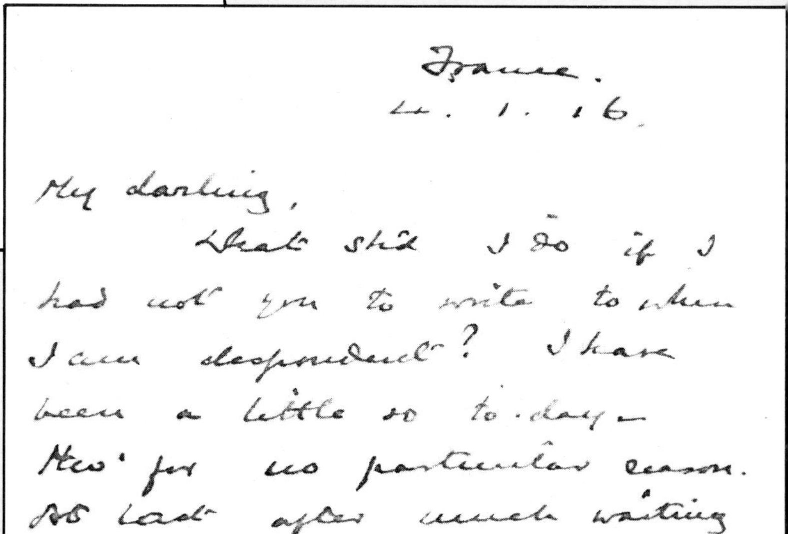

France.
4. 1. 16.

My darling,

What shd I do if I had not you to write to when I am despondent? I have been a little so to-day — tho' for no particular reason. At last after much waiting I have been made Colonel of the 6th Royal Scots Fusiliers; and tomorrow at noon I take over the command.

117

41. CROMWELL ROAD.

My Darling
        I miss you
terribly — I ache to see
you. When do you think
you will get a little
leave? Shall I come &
spend it with you in
Paris or will you come
home? I don't like to
make any request wh[ich]

118

During these dark months Clementine was Winston's chief source of informed news from the political world at home, of which she was a watchful and perceptive reporter. Although torn with anxiety for his personal safety and sharing much of his bitterness over the attitude of his erstwhile colleages and although angered by much ill-informed and unjust criticism, she managed to dominate these feelings and to give Winston sage, and at times nobly disinterested, advice. Through all these dark days she sustained Winston by her love, and her faith in his destiny: '. . . in your star I have confidence'.

But she herself often felt very low and depressed, and in one of her letters she sent him a transcription of the poem 'Up-hill' by Christina Rossetti, which begins:

Does the road wind up-hill all the
    way?
Yes, to the very end.
Will the day's journey take the whole
    long day?
From morn to night, my friend.

119

Winston is here photographed with his second-in-command, a young Scottish baronet, Sir Archibald Sinclair, who was a regular officer in the Life Guards. Since being in France, Winston had formed a warm friendship with 'Archie' Sinclair and this was to endure a lifetime. Later Sir Archibald entered politics, becoming Leader of the Liberal Party, and holding office in Churchill's Coalition Government.

120

Not all Clementine's news from home concerned politics. She, of course, told him all about the children, and about her canteen work, which was long and arduous.
Great family excitement was caused by her sister Nellie's marriage to Lieutenant-Colonel Bertram Romilly D.S.O. in early December 1915. Diana was bridesmaid, and Randolph and his cousin Johnnie, pages.

121

In March 1916, Winston had some leave. Here is a pleasant picture of him riding with Clementine in Rotten Row, Hyde Park. But his precious ten days were not all a time of relaxation and family life, as Clementine had hoped and planned, for Winston flung himself once more into political affairs. On 7 March he took part in the debate in the House of Commons on the Navy Estimates.

During the spring of 1917 Winston, who had been in touch with political friends at home, formed the resolve that the time had come for him to play his part in the affairs of the nation once more. During April he was with his battalion, going in and out of the line, but in early May the amalgamation of several battalions, due to heavy losses in the Scottish regiments, resulted in him having to give way to a senior colonel, and his connection with his battalion thus came naturally to an end. Churchill then sought, and was granted, permission to relinquish his rank and to return to England – where he saw his true role and destiny to lie.

Returned to the scene of home politics, Churchill joined the already considerable body of opposition (both in and out of Parliament) to the Government's conduct of the war. Winston Churchill made a formidable critic – not only on account of his own ability, but also because of his knowledge as a former minister, and his recent first-hand experience as a soldier in the field.

Asquith's position was weakened both by this open opposition, and also by internal machinations in his Government. In December 1916, Lloyd George succeeded Asquith as Prime Minister. But Conservative hostility still kept Churchill from office.

In the autumn of 1916, Winston and Clementine stayed for a weekend at Hackwood House near Basingstoke, then the home of Earl Curzon. The picture (above left) shows them on the front door steps. On the tennis court (above right), Clementine is with Arthur James Balfour; his friendship with the Churchills remained unaltered throughout all the vicissitudes of party strife: he was a Tory, and had succeeded Winston at the Admiralty in 1915 (Winston had been glad of this – since A.J.B. had always supported the concept of the Dardanelles plan). But it is interesting to remark upon the admirable urbanity of the world in which Winston and Clementine moved: Balfour had borne the brunt of Churchill's attack in the debate on the Naval Estimates that spring, and their host, too, Lord Curzon was a member of the Cabinet in the Government which was incurring Churchill's vigorous criticisms.

124

This is the portrait by Sir William Orpen painted in the summer of 1915, just after Churchill had
left the Admiralty. At that time, Clementine did not like the picture – perhaps because
it showed with too penetrating a painfulness the personal torment of those days following the
debacle of the Dardanelles: but in after years she was to think
it the best portrait ever painted of Winston.
In September 1916, the Dardanelles Commission started its sittings; Churchill gave evidence,
and himself questioned various witnesses. The Commission's First Report was published
in 1917, and did much to exonerate Churchill from the charges and criticisms which had been
levelled against him concerning that ill-fated operation, and which up to now
he had had to bear in silence. Later that same year, Lloyd George felt secure enough to ignore
the continuing hostility of certain Conservative ministers towards Churchill, and made him
Minister of Munitions. Now once more, Winston's energy and talents
were harnessed to the active service of his country.

The Sketch

No. 1323 — Vol. CII.   WEDNESDAY, JUNE 5. 1918   ONE SHILLING.

125

In the summer of 1918 a family event of great interest took place – Jennie Cornwallis-West (who
had divorced George Cornwallis-West in 1913) married again. And this time also
she married a man many years younger than herself – Mr Montagu Porch was forty while Jennie
was sixty-three. He was a member of the North Nigerian Civil Service, and they had
known each other and corresponded for several years. Not unnaturally, this event was the
cause of mixed feelings among Jennie's relations – including a degree of embarrassment.
But Winston and Jack and their wives joined in rejoicing with the inextinguishable Jennie – and
wished her joy with all their hearts. It is pleasant to record that, strange match
though it was, Jennie (who reverted to the style of Lady Randolph Churchill) was happy with
her Mr Porch, and he continued to be deeply devoted to her.

Winston is here witnessing the ceremonial entry of British troops into Lille in late October 1918. The officer in the foreground on the left is none other than Lieutenant-Colonel Bernard Montgomery, later Field Marshal Lord Montgomery of Alamein. This must have been the first time he and Winston Churchill met. From left to right, others in the picture are: (standing) Maréchal Foch; (sitting) W.S.C.; (standing) Millicent, Duchess of Sutherland (who had been running a hospital in Flanders); Eddie Marsh, W.S.C.'s Private Secretary.

126a

SPECIAL VICTORY NUMBER.   FINAL NIGHT EDITION.

ROYAL EXCHANGE ASSURANCE A.D. 1720

FIRE AND ACCIDENT INSURANCES.

The Globe

AND TRAVELLER. Founded 1803.

ROYAL EXCHANGE ASSURANCE A.D. 1720

LIFE AND MARINE INSURANCES.

No. 38,482.   MONDAY EVENING, NOV. 11, 1918.   ONE PENNY.

VICTORY!

GERMANY SURRENDERS.

OUR TERMS ACCEPTED TO-DAY.

127

On 15 November 1918, four days after the Armistice, Winston and Clementine's fourth child –
a girl – was born: they named her Marigold Frances. But, like all their children,
she had a 'pet' name. Diana's was 'the Gold-cream kitten' (and gold-cream exactly described her
subtle colouring then, as later in life). Randolph, on the whole a combative animal,
was less aptly known as 'the Rabbit'. Sarah, with her tawny mop of hair, was 'Bumblebee'.
Now Marigold, the darling of them all, became 'the Duckadilly'.

128

Winston and Clementine taking Sarah with them to watch a march-past of the Guards at
Buckingham Palace. With them is Sylvia Henley, Clementine's cousin.

After the Great War

Winston Churchill was successively Secretary of State for War (1919-21), and then Secretary of State for Colonies (1921-22), until the fall of Lloyd George's Coalition Government. The early 1920s saw Churchill move by degrees away from the Liberal Party (which had sunk into dismal disunity), back once more to the Conservative Party. The last obstacle to his reconciliation with the Conservatives was removed when they abandoned Protectionism. Clementine followed the reasoning of Winston's 'crossing the floor' of the House of Commons, and was to campaign energetically for him in the years to come: but she never made a very good Tory, and held deeply ingrained Liberal sympathies to the end of her life. In the General Election of 1924, Churchill was elected Member of Parliament for West Essex (Epping) – later re-named Wanstead and Woodford: a seat he was to hold as a Conservative for the forty more years of his parliamentary life. In Baldwin's second Government, Churchill was Chancellor of the Exchequer from 1924 to 1929. Although nearly all this time in office, Winston wrote and published (between 1923-29) *The World Crisis*: a history of the 1914-18 War in four volumes. In the General Election of 1929, the Conservatives failed to win an overall majority, and Stanley Baldwin resigned. Out of office Churchill entered on ten years in the political wilderness. With hindsight, these years have come to be regarded as the preparation for the role he would be called upon to play in the hour of Britain's greatest danger.

In 1919 Winston had been made Secretary of State for War, and some two years later, in 1921,
he was appointed Colonial Secretary. In March, soon after his appointment,
Winston accompanied by Clementine went to the Middle East. At the Cairo Conference
decisions were made for the settlement of frontiers and kingdoms in that region
after the convulsions of the war. Colonel T.E. Lawrence, the brilliant and charismatic
'Lawrence of Arabia', was Winston's chief adviser on Arab affairs, and became a firm friend.
Here, Winston and Clementine, accompanied by Gertrude Bell (the famous Orientalist,
traveller and writer) and Lawrence, are caught in true tourist pose beneath the Sphinx.

131

For the family, 1921 was destined to be a year of sadness and loss.
Shortly after Winston and Clementine returned from the Middle East in April, Clementine
learned of her brother's death in Paris: he had committed suicide. Bill was only
thirty-three, charming and debonair; there was no clue to the tragedy. Winston, too, had been
devoted to his brother-in-law, and shared Clementine's grief.
This picture of Bill, taken a year or two earlier, shows him with Clementine (left) and a friend.

132

At the end of June 1921 Lady Randolph died aged sixty-seven. She had tripped (wearing shoes with imprudently high heels) and fallen down a staircase, breaking an ankle. Presently gangrene set in, and her leg had to be amputated. She endured some painful weeks with characteristic pluck, and then died suddenly of a massive haemorrhage. Letters and tributes poured in, for Jennie, with her beauty and indomitable spirit, had become a legend in her own lifetime.

The snapshot (right) was taken a year or two before her death. But let us take leave of Jennie with the marvellous charcoal drawing by Sir John Sargent (above), showing her at the zenith of her triumphant beauty.

134

Jennie was buried at Bladon, in the churchyard where Lord Randolph already lay
and where, in time, their sons would join them. At the funeral
(left to right) are Winston, Jack, Johnnie (Jack's son), Oswald Frewen (Clara's son),
Mrs Moreton Frewen (Clara, Jennie's sister), Lady Leslie (Leonie, Jennie's sister),
Lady Gwendeline Churchill (Goonie, Jack's wife), Clementine and Sir John Leslie
(Leonie's husband). Winston loved his mother always with uncritical devotion.
Later he was to write of her that when he was a small child 'she shone for me like the
Evening Star'. Now, in answer to a letter of
condolence, Winston wrote: '. . . the wine of life was in her veins'.

135

The worst blow of all in this year of heavy tidings came at the end of August,
when Marigold (aged two years and nine months) died of septicaemia
of the throat. She was with the three other children and their governess
in lodgings by the sea at Broadstairs; they were all to join their parents later for
a family holiday. When it was apparent that the child was really ill,
her parents were sent for. They rushed to her, but tragically the dawn of the age
of antibiotics was too late to help 'the Duckadilly'. Both Winston
and Clementine were grief-stricken. Clementine buried Marigold deep in her
heart, and only very rarely spoke of her, but she
visited her grave, with its beautiful little monument by
Eric Gill, right up to within a year or two of her own death.

Christmas 1921: Sarah (seven), Randolph (ten) and Diana (twelve).

137

136

138

139

140

Summer holidays 1922. The family took a large house called Maryland (below)
at Frinton-on-Sea. Winston was a champion organizer and builder of sandcastles, and
children and grown-ups alike were mobilized. (Left to right) Winston – Commander-in-Chief;
Sarah; Clementine; the three gentlemen in ties – chauffeur and detectives;
Diana, and guarding the ramparts, Randolph.
The photograph (below, left) shows Randolph and Sarah with their 'other' cousins –
Nellie Romilly's boys, Giles (six) and Esmond (four).
The Romilly boys were known as 'the Lambs'. Their mother spoilt them enormously
and idolized them: their father had been badly wounded in the war, and was
somewhat remote from his children. 'The Lambs' were soon to become fairly unlamb-like.

141

142

Clementine was expecting another baby, and left the family party to return to London where on
15 September their fifth, and last, child was born: they called her Mary.

143

144

145

In 1920, Winston and Clementine had moved into a new London home – No. 2 Sussex Square, just to the north of Hyde Park. But for some time they had both yearned for what they called a 'country basket', and they had been on the look-out for something suitable. Moreover, a sudden and unlooked for legacy to Winston from a distant kinsman made the acquisition of a country house financially feasible.

One day in the summer of 1922, Winston saw a property near Westerham in Kent – Chartwell: he fell instantly and lastingly in love with the beautiful valley and its spring-fed lake, surrounded to the north and east by sheltering beech woods, and with a breathtaking view to the south across the verdant Weald of Kent, from the hilltop on which stands the house.

These photographs show Chartwell as it was in 1922 when Winston first acquired it. At first Clementine (then in the last months of her pregnancy) too was enthusiastic about it, but the house particularly posed problems – it was a mid-Victorian house, built around the core of a much older dwelling: it was covered with ivy, riddled with dry rot, and in a considerable state of dilapidation. It was after she had thoroughly investigated the condition and fundamental design of the house, that Clementine perceived several ineradicable faults, and also the extent of the work which would be necessary to make it habitable – and she took fright. Clementine also saw, with her more practical eye, that the garden and grounds were too big, and would swallow labour and money. All these difficulties and drawbacks she represented to Winston: and there she imagined the matter rested, and that nothing further would be done over the buying of Chartwell. Meanwhile, she was off to the seaside with the children to await the arrival of her baby.

But Winston was determined to have Chartwell: and he entered into negotiations to buy the property. His offer was accepted shortly after Mary's birth. Winston was convinced that Chartwell was the ideal country home for all the family; that the difficulties would be overcome, the shortcomings rectified, and that Clementine would come to love the place as much as he did – but this was never the case. And moreover, she was always to nurse feelings of resentment, which would surface from time to time, that Winston had been less than frank with her over the buying of Chartwell. But – the die having been cast – Clementine threw herself into the planning of the house and garden, and made the best of it all. But Chartwell was never to be for her the place of pleasure, fun, and unalloyed happiness it was from the beginning for Winston, and for all the forty years they were to live there.

146

October 1922 saw the fall of Lloyd George's Coalition Government: with the subsequent resignation
of among others, Churchill, Bonar Law formed a Conservative Government, and in November there
was a General Election. Meanwhile Winston had been taken ill, and operated on for appendicitis –
then a serious operation. He could not therefore go to his Dundee constituency until the final days of
the election campaign. Clementine, however, valiantly set forth for the North and, although Mary was
only six weeks old, took a leading part in the campaign, canvassing and speaking at rowdy meetings.
Here Winston is arriving for the last few days before Polling Day. One can see how frail he was,
and he is being borne by some of his supporters in a carrying chair; he had to
deliver most of his speeches sitting down. In the event his large majority was swept away – reflecting
the political tide in the country, where the Conservatives won by a
large majority. Freed from office, Winston could take a long convalescence, and the whole family
moved to Cannes where they took a villa for several months. Winston wryly
commented at this time that he was '. . . without
an office, without a seat, without a party, and without an appendix'.

148

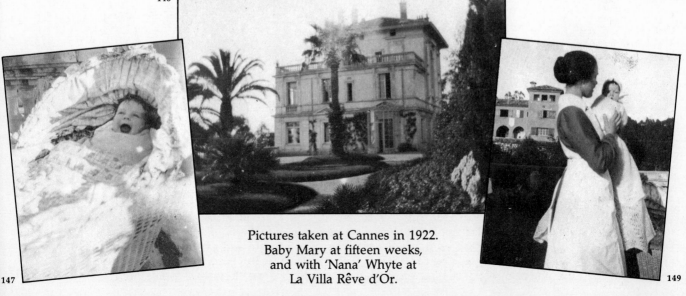

Pictures taken at Cannes in 1922.
Baby Mary at fifteen weeks,
and with 'Nana' Whyte at
La Villa Rêve d'Or.

147

149

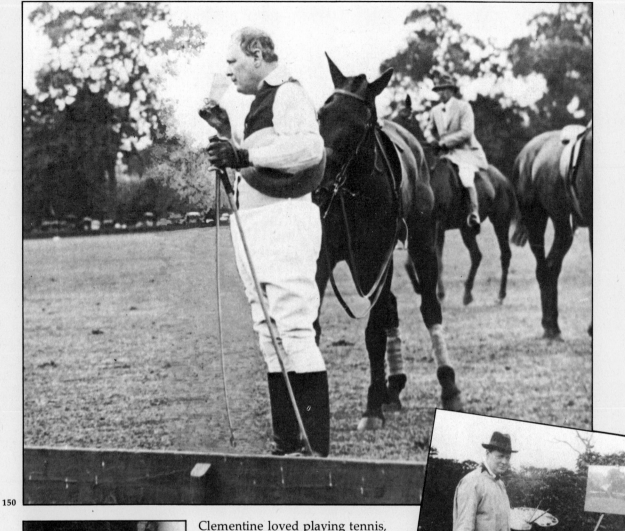

150

151

152

Clementine loved playing tennis, which she did extremely well. She was in great demand for country-house tournaments, where excellent tennis was often played. She was appreciated as a 'steady' partner. Here she is at Fairlawne, near Tonbridge in Kent, the home of the Cazalet family, where the standard was very high.

Although politics and writing had first claim on Winston's thoughts and time, there were other occupations and diversions – polo and painting. Winston had learned to play polo as a young cavalry officer in India. He still played in the 1920s, and kept his own ponies (I can just remember them out to grass at Chartwell). He gave up polo about 1926. This picture shows Winston taking a refresher during a break in a Lords v. Commons match in June 1922. Since he started to paint as an antidote to the anguish of the Dardanelles, painting had become a constant pleasure, preoccupation and companion. His paintings show that he can hardly ever have spent even a few days away from home without taking his paints . . . Here he is painting at Hartsbourne Manor, the home of Miss Maxine Elliott, the American-born actress; he also used sometimes to stay at her villa in the South of France, where he delighted to paint, and found many sunlit scenes.

153

154

155

Above, Winston and myself aged two, at Chartwell. Left, Diana being very protective to 'baby Mary'. Below: What a fashion plate! – Winston and Clementine, 1923.

156

157

Here are somewhat jollier election photographs than the last one!
After 1922, when he was defeated at Dundee, Winston
moved by degrees and through several elections from the
Liberal Party to (once more) the Conservative Party. In the
General Election following the fall of the Labour Government in
October 1924 he won West Essex (Epping). He was
to remain the Conservative member for this constituency (later
renamed the Wanstead and Woodford Division of Essex)
for the remaining forty years of his political life.
Above, he and Clementine are being driven on a tour of the
constituency by one of their supporters – Mr Claud F. Goddard –
in his coach and four. Left, electioneering in the rain.
In Stanley Baldwin's new government Winston Churchill
was made Chancellor of the Exchequer (until 1929).
So the Churchills moved into No. 11 Downing Street,
the Chancellor's official residence.

158

In his first Budget in April 1925, Churchill took Britain back onto the Gold Standard. He also lopped 6d off Income Tax – thereby reducing it to four shillings! Clementine took Randolph (aged thirteen) and Diana (fifteen) to hear their father's speech in the House of Commons.

159

My father was usually chauffeur-driven; and during any journey of length he would, more often than not, work at proofs or speeches, frequently dictating to his secretary, who had to be able to take shorthand 'in motion' and be immune to both swaying and a close atmosphere heavily laden with cigar smoke!
In this picture, taken in 1925, Winston's companion is Sir Philip Cunliffe-Lister (later the Earl of Swinton), a friend and colleague. As a cabinet minister in the 1930s he did his utmost to promote the re-arming of Britain in spite of tepid government policy. Sitting behind is Detective-Sergeant (later Inspector) W.H. Thompson of the Special Branch, Scotland Yard. He was detailed to guard Churchill from 1920, when the Irish troubles were particularly menacing to government ministers. Winston was a target, being deeply involved in the negotiations which led up to partition and the Government of Ireland Act 1920. Thompson left Churchill in 1932, but at the outbreak of war in 1939 he was recalled from retirement, and once more became his personal bodyguard, remaining with him until 1945.

Blanche Hozier and Jock

69 years old. 12 years old.

160

At the end of March 1925, Lady Blanche Hozier (Clementine's mother) died
at the age of seventy-three.

Despite unhappy memories of her adored Kitty's death there, Lady Blanche had
returned some years later to Dieppe and had bought a charming house
with a garden – 16 rue des Fontaines, and made it her home. Blanche Hozier was
greatly addicted both to French life and to gambling! She was able to indulge
this taste to the full, for Dieppe had a casino. If she was in debt,
Lady Blanche would let her house, and live for a time in a *pension* or modest hotel,
in order to recoup her losses! She was in fact living in an hotel on the
seafront (within easy walking distance of the casino) when she fell ill.

Both Clementine and Nellie went at once to be with their mother.

Before her marriage Clementine did not have an easy relationship with her mother –
their natures were very different. Nellie was much more attuned to her
mother's personality. But Winston liked and got on with his mother-in-law from the
beginning, and she reciprocated his affection. And from the time of
her marriage Clementine's relationship with her mother greatly improved – although
they could never spend too much time together!

When Lady Blanche was dying, Winston wrote a warm and understanding letter to
Clementine: 'My darling I grieve for you . . . the loss of a mother severs a chord
in the heart and makes life seem lonely & its duration fleeting . . .
I greatly admired & liked your mother. She was an ideal mother-in-law. Never shall I
allow that relationship to be spoken of with mockery – for her sake . . .'

This picture of Lady Blanche Hozier (so charmingly inscribed in her own hand)
was taken some four years before she died.

In January 1927 Winston went to Italy. As it was the Christmas holidays, he took Randolph with him (Randolph was at school at Eton). While in Rome they did some sightseeing. Here Winston and Randolph, with Jack Churchill behind, are arriving at the Thermae of Caracalla. I think Randolph must be wearing his first trilby! During his visit to Rome, Winston saw Signor Mussolini, the fascist leader, and premier since 1922.

During the nine-day General Strike in 1926 which brought the country to the brink of civil strife, Churchill was foremost in organising an emergency Government broadsheet.

164

During the years between the two World Wars Winston and Clementine went frequently to France, mostly staying with English friends who had houses
there. Here is Winston at Deauville, in August 1927, emerging from the sea.

165

166

Here is a picture of Winston with his kinsman and great friend, Sunny Marlborough, taken at Blenheim by Sunny's second wife, Gladys Deacon (seen in the heyday of her beauty, above right), whom he had married in 1921. Although they had separated in 1906, Sunny and Consuelo were not actually divorced until 1921. Consuelo also remarried – to a Frenchman, Colonel Jacques Balsan. When Sunny Marlborough died in 1934 at the age of sixty-three from cancer, Winston felt deeply bereft.

167

Christmas at Chartwell was always a glorious feast. The same party usually assembled: Winston and Clementine and their four children; Jack and Goonie, with Johnnie, Peregrine and Clarissa (born in 1920); Bertram and Nellie Romilly with Giles and Esmond. The only 'outsiders' were Professor Lindemann ('The Prof . . . later Lord Cherwell) and sometimes Eddie Marsh. The Christmas and New Year of 1927-8 was the time of the Great Snow. The older children constructed a marvellous igloo; there was a snowman, tobogganning, and skating on the lake. (168) Clementine with 'The Prof'; (169) Mary tobogganning, watched by Sarah; (170) Clementine with Randolph; (171) Winston with our snowman!

168

169

170

171

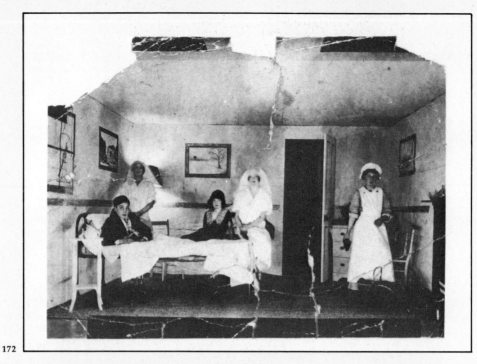

172

Amateur theatricals were also a feature of the Christmas holidays at Chartwell. The dining-room made a splendid theatre, with its dividing curtains already in position.
Here is a scene from one of the productions. Dramatis personae, left to right: Johnnie is the patient; behind him is 'nurse' Randolph; Sarah is the visitor sitting on the patient's toes; behind her is 'nurse' Diana. Peregrine is the ward maid to the right.

173

Winston and Clementine's visits to France in the summer were occupied with painting and writing (and some gambling) for him, and tennis for her. But often in January and February they would stay with the Duke of Westminster and hunt wild boar with his hounds. Here Winston, Clementine and Randolph are out with the hounds in the Forest of Allongy, near Bourges.
The Duke of Westminster, 'Bendor' (left): one of Winston's greatest friends, he was an incomparable host and the most engaging of companions. Winston and Clementine stayed with him often, in France, and at home at Eaton Hall near Chester, or in Scotland at Lochmore, Sutherland.

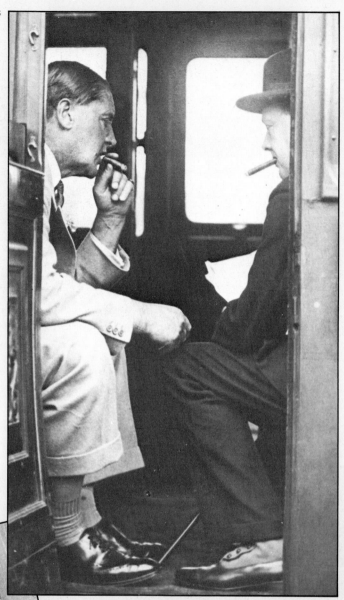

Here is Winston deep in conversation with one of his greatest friends and cronies – the Earl of Birkenhead (F. E. Smith). Tory politician and one of the most brilliant advocates of his day, he was successively Solicitor-General, Attorney-General and then Lord Chancellor (1919-22). Winston and 'F.E.' had first met when they were fierce political opponents before the First World War; but party politics had made no difference to their friendship. Clementine disapproved of F.E., and thought he was a bad influence on Winston – but she was very fond of his wife, Margaret (with Winston, left). The families were intertwined: F.E. was Randolph's godfather, and Freddie Furneaux (his only son) and two daughters, Eleanor and Pamela, were great friends of Diana and Randolph. When F.E. died aged only fifty-eight in 1930, Winston, with Sunny Marlborough (above) at the funeral, was deeply grieved. Gladys Marlborough cut this picture out of a newspaper or magazine and stuck it in her album. Clementine wrote to Margaret Birkenhead immediately after his death: 'Last night Winston wept for his friend. He said several times "I feel so lonely".'

178

In spite of a full political life and ministerial office, Winston still found time to engage in major
works of construction at Chartwell: a dam; a swimming pool; and the building
(largely with his own hands) of the red brick wall to surround the large vegetable garden.
Here he is hard at work with Sarah (aged fourteen) as bricklayer's mate.

179

Winston with Clementine, Sarah (fourteen), and Randolph (seventeen) who had gone up to
Oxford at the beginning of this year, on their way to the House of Commons on 15 April 1929,
where Winston was to present his fifth (and last) Budget. Also in the picture are
(left) Detective-Sergeant Thompson and, just behind him in top hat,
Mr (later Sir) Robert Boothby M.P., Winston's Parliamentary Private Secretary.
The following month there was a General Election, at which the Conservative Party was
defeated and Ramsay Macdonald formed his second Labour administration. Out of office,
Winston and his family moved from the Chancellor's official residence – 11 Downing Street –
and concentrated their forces at Chartwell.

In December 1929, Winston was installed as Chancellor of Bristol
University: it was an appointment by which he set much store, and
which he held until his death. Here is Winston, in his robes and (above)
unceremoniously borne aloft by students.

180

181

182

183

Here are two pictures of Winston and Clementine at sporting occasions. Winston (with even for
him, unusual headgear) is seen with Mlle Coco Chanel, the famous couturiere, at a shoot near
Eaton Hall, Chester, where they were among the guests of the Duke of Westminster ('Bendor').
A few months later – again staying at Eaton Hall (this time for the Grand National) –
Clementine is with Sunny Marlborough.

184

Released from ministerial cares and duties, Winston planned an extensive tour of Canada
and the USA. The party would consist of himself, Clementine, Randolph,
his brother Jack Churchill and his son Johnnie. Clementine had been operated on for
tonsils earlier in the summer and, although largely recovered, was not strong
enough in the event to undertake a long and strenuous journey. The party left in early August.
Here they are in Calgary, Alberta.

185

During this tour, which included much enjoyable sightseeing, Winston made speeches in most of
the cities he visited, and called upon local notabilities. In September
the party crossed (by way of the Rockies) into the United States.
They were guests at a Hollywood luncheon given by Louis B. Mayer. In this photograph are
(left to right) Randolph Churchill, William Randolph Hearst, Winston, Louis B. Mayer, (?),
Jack Churchill, (?), and Johnnie.

Winston took twenty-five minutes to land this
188lb swordfish off Catalina Island, California.
Winston was always keen on dashing hats,
and after this visit to California he almost
invariably wore a 'cowboy' hat (left) when at
home on his own 'ranch', or when painting.

Years in the wilderness

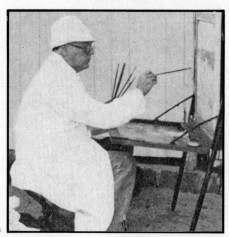

188

During the three months Winston was on his travels in North America during the early autumn of 1929, speaking, meeting people and sightseeing had not been his only occupations: the stock markets were booming – and Winston (profiting from expert advice) engaged in speculation. He was actually in New York in early October when the great crash of the American stock market occurred, in which he lost what was for him, a small fortune. This, then, was the unpalatable news with which he had to greet Clementine on his return home in the last week of October. So the Churchills entered the decade of the 1930s in somewhat muted vein. They did not acquire a new London house, but, for a year of two after the 'crash', either stayed in hotels or rented houses for short periods. After 1931, however, they bought the lease of the top two floors of No. 11 Morpeth Mansions, an apartment block behind Westminster Cathedral: this was to be their London home until the outbreak of the war.

Despite the severe setback to his fortunes Winston was, by his brilliance and industry, able to keep his family, and live in style and comfort at his beloved Chartwell, through his writings. At times it was a near-run thing between bills and books, and the fragility of the economic raft on which they lived was a cause of great anxiety to Clementine, and was certainly the main reason why her enjoyment of Chartwell was dimmed. Meanwhile, as the new decade opened, the rift between Winston and the main body of Conservative thought was beginning to widen.

Apart from his major works, the most notable in the 1930s being the monumental *Life* of his
ancestor, John, Duke of Marlborough, in four volumes, Churchill poured forth speeches,
and newspaper and magazine articles. Chartwell was not only his home and his 'playground',
it was his 'factory' – and the lights burned late into the night. There were always two secretaries
employed for his work alone, in order to cope with the late-night 'shifts',
and the great volume of his literary output and correspondence.
Despite his deep involvement in public events, Winston continued to work away at his writings.
This picture of Winston in his study at Chartwell was taken in 1939. In 1938, the
fourth and last volume of his *Life* of Marlborough had been published; he had now started on a
new literary venture, a *History of the English-Speaking Peoples*. This work was destined
to be put aside for several years: it was finally published during the 1950s.

Chartwell was ever and always the focus of Winston and Clementine's family and social life. Those who stayed for week-ends were nearly always members of the family or close cronies such as Professor Lindemann or Brendan Bracken. But since Chartwell was only an hour from London, many were the friends, colleagues and acquaintances who came for the day; and it was a company as varied as it was fascinating.

The 1930s marked that decade which, in terms of Winston Churchill's life, has come to be called 'The Wilderness Years'. The controversies centring upon the India Bill were soon to be eclipsed by a more deadly dilemma: how to make those who did not want to hear, listen to the distant but distinct rumbles of thunder; and how to open the eyes of the purblind to see the darkening and ominous clouds rolling up on an ever less distant horizon. As the decade wore on, the band of visitors to Chartwell was increased by a small but steady to-ing and fro-ing of courageous men from the armed forces and the administration who, seeing the danger to the country, took risks with their own careers and reputations to fuel the power of seemingly the one man who could do something to awaken Britain both to the dangers in Europe inherent in the rise of Hitler and Nazi power, and the weak state of this country's defences. Churchill and his small band of like-minded men and women waged a constant – and apparently fruitless – battle against apathy and an unwillingness to look facts in the face which, starting with the government, had spread through the nation.

Kept at arm's length by his Party, and his warnings largely unheeded by the greater number of his countrymen, even Winston Churchill's doughty determination and gallant spirit was not proof against moments of depression and near despair. On a domestic level, Chartwell was to prove the financial burden Clementine had from the first predicted it would be. Now that we know how the tale unfolded, it makes curious reading to find Winston writing to Clementine in February 1937 to tell her that if a good price were to be offered for Chartwell, he would accept it, 'having regard to the fact that our children are almost all flown, and *my life is probably in its closing decade*'. When he wrote those words, Winston Churchill was in his sixty-third year: he had twenty-eight more years of life – and the hour of his greatest achievement was yet to come.

One of those with whom Winston had made friends during his visit to Hollywood in 1929 was Charlie Chaplin, who came to visit him at Chartwell in July 1931. The group by the front door is (left to right): my pug-dog 'Mr Punch'; Tom Mitford (Clementine's cousin, and great friend of Diana and Randolph. He was the only brother of the famous Mitford sisters, and was killed in Burma in 1945); Winston; (behind left): Freddie Birkenhead (Earl of Birkenhead – F.E.'s son. He became a distinguished writer and historian); Clementine; Diana (now twenty-two); Randolph (twenty); Charlie Chaplin. The picture on the right is of Lawrence of Arabia, in his uniform as Aircraftman Shaw. After all his adventures he chose to serve in the ranks of the Royal Air Force, assuming the name of Shaw. A strange, charismatic figure, he visited Churchill regularly until his death in 1935.

Above: Professor F.W. Lindemann (later Viscount Cherwell) – always known as 'The Prof'. Of American-Alsatian extraction, he was a brilliant scientist, and for over forty years Winston's close friend and scientific mentor; he could explain the most abstruse scientific propositions in simple terms. He was a bachelor, a strict vegetarian and teetotaller – and a championship tennis player. Clementine was devoted to him, and he was constantly at Chartwell.

Above, Winston with Professor Einstein in the rose garden in the 1930s. Left, Major (later Sir) Desmond Morton; a neighbour of Edenbridge, he was a constant visitor. Involved in Economic Intelligence, he primed Winston with invaluable information. Right, Brendan (later Viscount) Bracken, one of Winston's most faithful friends and political supporters. His outlandish appearance – carrot hair and spectacles like gig-lamps – was matched by an equally unusual mind and personality.

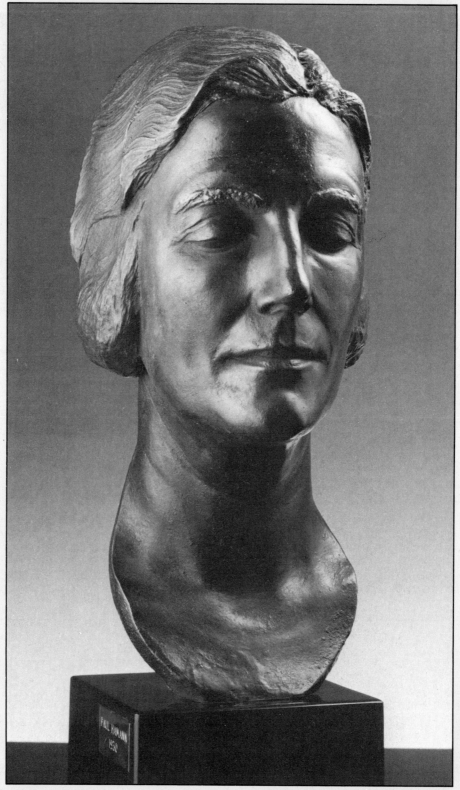

197

About 1930, Clementine had a life mask taken by Paul Hamann, a German artist who was
working in London at that time. I was seven, and I remember being terror-stricken
when I saw my mother's head and neck encased in thick layers of gluey plaster: I was sure she
was being suffocated, despite straws placed in her nostrils!
Many years later Paul Hamann's widow, who had left Germany in the early 1930s
and who eventually came to live in England, contacted me, and recently I have had
the plaster mask cast in bronze. I find it very beautiful, and it shows the purity and classical
quality of my mother's features, which were to endure into her old age.

During these next few years, the political question which was to occupy a great part of Churchill's thought and activity was the future government and constitutional status of India. And it was over this question that deep differences arose between him and Stanley Baldwin, finally marked by Churchill's resignation, in January 1931, from the Conservative Business Committee (the equivalent of today's Shadow Cabinet). This was to cost Churchill a place in the National Government which was formed in August of that year. There was a General Election two months later, in October, with a landslide victory for the National Government. Winston himself was ever safe and secure in his Epping constituency.

With no governmental ties, Winston undertook a lecture tour in the United States. Accompanied by Clementine and Diana, he sailed for New York in early December 1931. They had only been in New York a few days when Winston, crossing the road with insufficient prudence, was bowled over by a taxi-cab. Fortunately he was wearing a heavy fur-lined overcoat, or he might easily have been killed; as it was, he suffered severe shock and considerable injury.

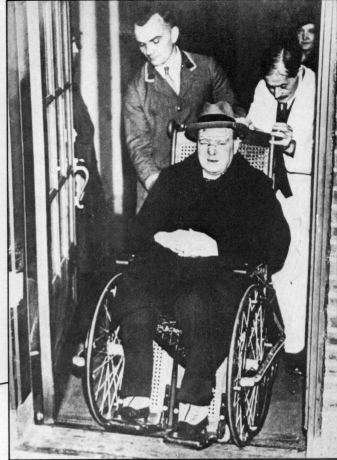

198

Nassau - Bahamas.
January 22. 1932

It was nice of Jan to telegraph
about Winston. He is much
better. This is such a heavenly
climate & the Temperature of it is 74°C.
The sea is turquoise
Clementine B.H.C.

199

Released from hospital, albeit in a somewhat fragile state, Winston spent Christmas in a hotel in New York with Clementine and Diana. On 31 December he was well enough to travel to Nassau for a convalescence in the sunshine. Here we see him leaving hospital – rather battered – in a wheel-chair. Clementine(left)here gives a good report of Winston's recovery to a friend. But some ten days earlier she had written to Randolph in a somewhat depressed vein; Winston was much cast down by the slowness of his recovery, and was evidently low in spirits, for Clementine wrote: 'Last night he was very sad & said that he had now in the last 2 years had 3 very heavy blows. First the loss of all that money in the crash, then the loss of his political position in the Conservative Party and now this terrible physical injury – He said he did not think he would ever recover completely from the three events...'

While they were in New York on this otherwise ill-fated expedition, Clementine was photographed by Cecil Beaton.

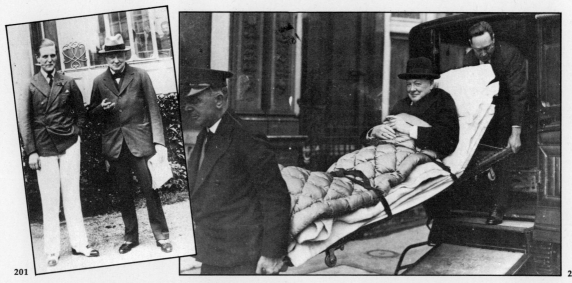

201

202

Winston was deeply engaged in writing the *Life* of his great ancestor John, Duke of Marlborough, and in the late summer of 1932 he set out to visit the most famous of Marlborough's battlefields – Ramillies, Oudenarde and Malplaquet; then he followed the line of Marlborough's army's epic march across Europe to Blenheim. With him as companions were Clementine, Randolph, Sarah, and 'the Prof', and Colonel Pakenham-Walsh, the military historian, who was their guide and mentor. Here are Winston and Randolph. Winston looks as if he is grasping some galley-proofs. Note the fashions in footwear: Randolph wears brown and white brogues (vulgarly known as 'co-respondents'!), while Winston is wearing spats.
But 1931 and 1932 were not lucky years health-wise for Winston. Arrived in Salzburg in early September after a month's travelling, Winston was admitted to a nursing-home suffering from paratyphoid. After about a fortnight he was well enough to go home to England. A few days after his return to Chartwell he had a sudden haemorrhage, and had to be rushed to a nursing-home in London. The picture shows Winston being carried from an ambulance, having been released from the nursing-home. He made a good recovery eventually, but for a time the illness much weakened him.

203

In December 1932, Diana married John Milner Bailey, the son of Sir Abe Bailey, the South African magnate and a friend of Winston's. Here Diana and her father are leaving Morpeth Mansions for her marriage at St Margaret's, Westminster. The marriage was unhappy, and Diana divorced John Bailey in 1935. They had no children.

1933 was a year of significant events: the gale of the India controversy was blowing at full force, but there were other preoccupations too: unemployment figures in Great Britain reached a peak of three million; in Germany, Hitler became Chancellor; at Oxford, in the Union, a motion that 'This House will in no circumstances fight for King and Country' was carried by a large majority – though a few years later many of those taking part in the debate would be fighter pilots; in October, Germany withdrew from the League of Nations. And all the while, Churchill continued to repeat his warnings of Britain's inadequate defences.

204

But on the family front life rolled on merrily enough. 1933 was the year Sarah 'came out'. The party we see (apparently sunk in deep gloom) consists of Sarah, Clementine and Winston, setting out for Buckingham Palace for Sarah to be presented at the first Court of the season in May. The white fluffy appendages in the ladies' hair are 'Prince of Wales' feathers, which were *de rigueur* at Presentation parties. Note also the ostrich feather fans – a must. 'Coming out' was a marathon: neither Sarah's nor Clementine's heart was in it – but they stuck it out. Clementine wrote to a friend that she found her fellow mothers 'really rather a depressing back-biting tribe & I have to sit for hours with them on the Chaperons' Bench. I'm thinking of taking a cookery book to Balls. I could be hunting up tasty recipes . . .'

205 206

Chartwell life had many aspects: here Clementine is hard at it, playing bezique with her
brother-in-law, Jack Churchill. Note: it must have been a bit chilly – Clementine
has a rug around her knees; 'Mr Punch' the pug dog can be
seen extreme right; and (right) Clementine swimming in the pool (devised and largely
constructed by Winston) at Chartwell, summer 1933.

207 208

Sarah escaped with the minimum respectable attendance at debutante functions: she preferred
mooning about listening to the gramophone; her real ambition was to
dance professionally, and she persuaded her parents with a good deal of difficulty to let her
go to a dancing school. (Left, Sarah is second in the right-hand file.) In the summer
of 1933 or 1934 some of the girls from the dancing school formed a troupe of dancers,
'The KitKat Players', and they came to Chartwell and gave several performances on the lawn.

1933 marked Winston and Clementine's Silver Wedding. A group of their friends joined in giving them a conversation piece . . . to be painted by William Nicholson. Thus began a friendship which brought great joy and enrichment – certainly to the Churchills. In order to paint the picture, William Nicholson came frequently to Chartwell and was a most welcome and diverting friend. Sittings apart, he painted many enchanting pictures at Chartwell and was a regular guest in the summers up to the war.

As some wit remarked: 'Everything is right about this picture, except of course Winston and Clementine never had breakfast together!' This is roughly true. But apart from this flight of poetic (or painter's) licence, Nicholson has caught my parents' attitudes and likenesses very well, and the picture, for me, evokes all the delight of that dining room on a sunny day, with the garden door open, one of my bantams strolling in to pick up the crumbs, and the cat making himself at home! It also appears as a colour frontispiece in this album. Right, Tango, our beautiful tangerine cat drawn by William Nicholson.

211

Winston's study then, as now, is the very heart of Chartwell; it is also the oldest part of the
house, and Philip Tilden, the architect who re-made Chartwell for the Churchills, caused the
ceiling of the room to be removed, revealing the beams and rafters of the earlier house.
Winston loved this room and he spent many long hours working here – reading, or correcting
his proofs, or (while padding up and down) dictating by the hour. On the left
is the 'working bench', designed by Winston and made in plain deal by the local carpenter.
It had two tiers (the top one on a slope), and stood on top of a wooden chest. Here documents,
source books, and galley-proofs could all be laid out for easy inspection.

Winston loved going to the South of France: there he painted to his heart's content – and of course he always took his work, the book-of-the-moment. But Clementine found the company on the whole tedious, and unlike Winston she had no absorbing hobby; she therefore often did not go with him to the Riviera. But in the summer of 1934 they both went on a holiday which managed to combine all the things they both enjoyed: they went on a Mediterranean cruise in the *Rosaura*, the yacht of their host, Lord Moyne (Walter Guinness . . . a former Financial Secretary to the Treasury, and a most intelligent and agreeable man. In November 1944 he was assassinated by the Jewish extremist Stern Gang while he was Deputy Minister of State in Cairo). They were away a month, visiting Athens and Cyprus, the southern coast of Turkey, Palmyra, Damascus and Jerusalem. Before they rejoined the yacht at Alexandria, Winston and Clementine had seen Jericho, Amman and Petra, and had revisited Cairo.

The Mediterranean cruise which both Winston and Clementine had so greatly enjoyed had given Clementine a taste for exotic and interesting travel. Later that same year Lord Moyne again invited them to join him on a voyage in *Rosaura*, seen in the top picture. This time the journey was to be to the ends of the earth: Walter Moyne was setting out for the island of Komodo, one of the Lesser Sunda Islands of Indonesia (then the Dutch East Indies), to endeavour to capture alive for the London Zoo some of the huge dragon-like monitor lizards which inhabit that island. The voyage was expected to last at least four months, and so it was really out of the question for Winston to accept this exciting invitation: he was in full flight writing his *Life* of Marlborough, quite apart from all his political activities – nor could he have borne to be so far from the hub of events for so long. But Winston realized that this was the chance of a lifetime for Clementine – so reluctantly, but lovingly, he let her go.

Clementine left London to join *Rosaura* just before Christmas 1934. We all went to Victoria Station to wave her off; in her first letter home to Winston she wrote: 'You all looked so sweet and beautiful standing there, and I thought how fortunate I am to have such a family. Do not be vexed with your vagabond cat. She has gone off towards the jungle with her tail in the air, but she will return presently to her basket and curl down comfortably . . .'

During the four months of her voyaging, Clementine was to traverse 30,000 miles of water! She was a wonderful correspondent, writing long, animated letters home. She revelled in it all – writing from an unexplored estuary along the south coast of New Guinea: 'This is the "genuine article"! uncharted seas, unexplored territory, stark naked savages.' Winston responded from a bleak British winter scene. He was busy – books, politics, and major works at Chartwell kept him occupied every waking hour, but he missed her: '. . . it makes one gasp to look at the map and see what enormous distances you have covered since I saw the last of your dear waving hand at Victoria Station; and it depresses me to feel the *weight* of all that space pressing down upon us both,' he wrote. And for all the excitements and pleasures of her travels Clementine missed him too, and very warm and loving were the letters traversing the vast tracts of ocean which separated them. Clementine wrote to Winston: 'Since Noumea we have been crossing the trackless ocean calling at various islands. We are quite out of touch, the waters round some of these islands are uncharted, they are surrounded by cruel coral reefs and often no bottom can be found . . .' Left, one of the Komodo 'dragons' which they had travelled so far to obtain. The lizards become more dragon-like with age, and can grow to twelve feet long; this is a young specimen. During the voyage, Lord Moyne is seen (bottom, far left) receiving some animated information from a local inhabitant. And (bottom left), a bathing party in somewhat makeshift swimming pool (Clementine is in the centre). All the family kept Clementine posted about our individual activities, and in addition to news about all of us, Winston kept her abreast of events on the political scene. However far from home, Clementine never lost interest in what was afoot politically, and avidly read out-of-date copies of *The Times* whenever she was in port. But the account of the works undertaken by Winston at Chartwell that winter of her absence, comprises a major saga in itself.

The two big projects were the excavation of a ha-ha to the north of the swimming pool (providing an unbroken line across the valley), and the severing of a narrow neck of land, thus turning the peninsula on the lower lake into a romantic island. To achieve these not insignificant engineering projects a mechanical digger had been hired. Winston had been assured that the miraculous monster could complete both operations in two weeks, at a cost of £25. Unfortunately, due to a series of unexpected difficulties (not least the sopping condition of the ground), the digger was at Chartwell for a good two months! Winston sent faithful accounts of the various setbacks and calamities which attended these operations – including snapshots, which as one can see give the impression that the hitherto verdant valley at Chartwell could well have served as a set for filming scenes from 'All Quiet on the Western Front'! Poor Clementine, all those miles away, must have been filled with consternation.

However, by the time she arrived home to tumultuous family rejoicings the worst depredations of the digger had been tidied up, and spring grass was beginning to carpet the mud.

Winston (below) is seen surveying the depredations of the digger which is excavating the ha-ha. The railway lines to the left carried skips full of unwanted earth away from the site. The faint figure marked 'P' (pig) in Winston's own hand is himself. This muddy scene shows the peninsula being made into an island.

218

Clementine arrived home from her travels just as the celebrations for the Silver Jubilee of King George V and Queen Mary were about to begin. Here I am (thirteen, and very much excited) going to Westminster Hall with my parents to witness the King and Queen receiving loyal addresses from both Houses of Parliament on 9 May 1935. On the left is Clementine's cousin, Maryott Whyte. She was a trained Norland Nurse who had come to look after the children after Marigold's death. She was my nannie (I called her 'Nana'), then governess, then 'duenna': she was a great feature of all our lives, and only went into retirement when I left home in the war.

219

On 16 September 1935, Diana married Duncan Sandys, whom she had met earlier that year. He was a clever up-and-coming diplomat, but he had left the Foreign Office in order to go into politics and had been elected Conservative member for Norwood in March 1935. We were all glad to see Diana happy again, and Duncan was to become close to his father-in-law politically.

220

King George died on 20 January 1936. The Prince of Wales, who ascended the throne aged forty-two, was to reign for less than twelve months. He was a beloved and popular figure, and millions throughout the Commonwealth were deeply affected by his Abdication in December 1936. In the controversy that raged, Winston stood loyally by the King, for whom he had a real affection. Below, King Edward VIII at the Cenotaph, 11 November. Below left, Winston leaves Fort Belvedere after lunching with the King on 11 December – the day of the Abdication.

221

MISS CHURCHILL'S VISIT TO U.S.

To Appear In Vic Oliver Show

MISS Sarah Churchill, the younger daughter of Mr. and Mrs. Winston Churchill, who is 21 and made her stage début in the chorus of ~~Sun,"~~ at the

Sarah started her stage career as one of C.B. Cochran's 'Young Ladies', in the revue *Follow the Sun* in 1935. Her parents were not reconciled to her being 'on the stage' – let alone as a chorus girl! But more was in store: Sarah fell in love with the star of the show, Vic Oliver, a gifted Viennese, seventeen years her elder, and twice married. Sarah did her utmost to persuade her parents to give their blessing to her marrying Vic: but finally she left without warning to join him in America in September 1936. The press made the most of all this. Left, Sarah going aboard the *Bremen* at Southampton, carrying a doll mascot. Below, Sarah and Vic together soon after her arrival: they were married in New York on Christmas Eve 1936.

225

Many and various are the demands made upon the wives of Members of Parliament! Here is Clementine opening the bowling for the 'Lyons Girls' cricket team who were playing the Woodford Police Athletic Club in September 1936.

My mother was both energetic and enterprising – at the age of fifty she decided to take up ski-ing! During the three peacetime Christmas holidays that remained, therefore, she took me either to Austria or Switzerland for two or three weeks. When I had to return to school she used to stay on for a little while, usually joining up with friends. This photograph of her was taken outside the Palace Hotel, St Moritz, January 1937, after I had been despatched home; on the back she has written to me: 'Don't be alarmed, I haven't bought this dog – he belongs to the photographer!'

226

227

Drinks in the sunshine . . . but where? I cannot identify the place. Clementine had dated it 1937,
and had marked in the names in her own hand. Left to right, sitting: Clementine;
Mr Somerset Maugham (to whom she was very partial); centre foreground, Lady Juliet Duff;
behind her, Dr Kommer; Venetia Montagu.

On 30 November 1937 it was Winston's
sixty-third birthday. He
was at Chartwell – Clementine in
London; she sent him this telegram.

POST
OFFICE
GREETINGS TELEGRAM

WESTERHAM
30 NO
37
KENT

7.35   London. T.

winston churchill chartwell.
                            westerham.
Many Happy Returns. My Darling one.
and may your star rise

        Clemmie

Throughout 1938 the tension in political and public life was gradually building up. March saw the Anschluss – Austria swallowed by the German Reich; and, as the spring and summer wore on, Germany exerted ever-increasing pressure on Czechoslovakia over the Sudeten German problem.

The Munich Agreement in September was hailed by the majority of the population as a pledge and a promise of 'peace in our time'. But for those who thought like Churchill – and their number and influence had been growing for some time – it was only a breathing space bought at a high and shameful price.

During 1938 Clementine had not been in very good health, and in addition to physical aches and pains, the strains of politics and the pace of her life were telling on her; so it seemed a golden opportunity to 'recharge her batteries' when Walter Moyne once more invited her to go for a journey on board *Rosaura*. This time, however, the purpose as well as the destination of the voyage were very different: Lord Moyne had been appointed Chairman of the Royal Commission which had been set up to enquire into the social conditions in the West Indies, so he was bound for the Caribbean, taking on board with him members of the Commission and a few personal guests.

Clementine left England to join the party in *Rosaura* (which was already in the Caribbean) at the end of November. As before, she enjoyed being at sea, and the beauty and interest of the various islands they visited thrilled her. She also took a great interest in the work of the Commission and penned some fiery missives home inveighing against the prevailing social conditions in the islands.

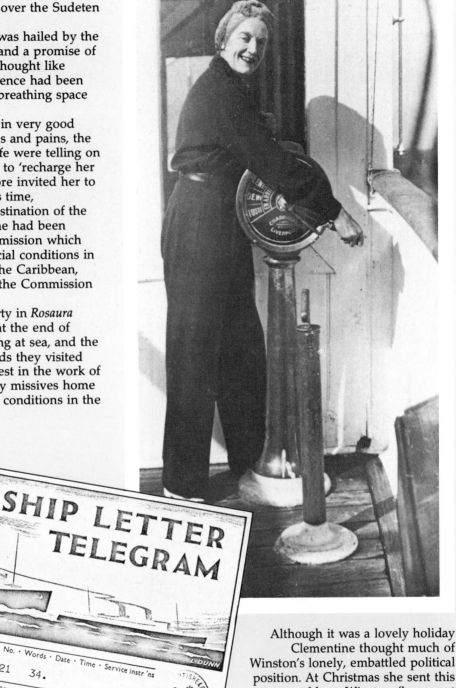

229

Although it was a lovely holiday Clementine thought much of Winston's lonely, embattled political position. At Christmas she sent this cable to Winston (he was at Blenheim with the stay-at-homes). Clementine was obviously homesick; moreover, there was political friction between fellow guests on board. Finally, at the end of January, she decided not to stay her time out but to head for home. Clementine sailed from Barbados in the *Cuba*, which happened to be in port at the time, and arrived back in England in the first week of February.

230

232

In December 1938 the London Zoo
received their first giant panda, Ming.
Great was the interest and
excitement; but the public had to
wait while Ming remained in
quarantine. Winston was much taken
with the photographs of Ming, and
was allowed a private audience
through the courtesy of the then
President of the Zoological Society,
Sir Julian Huxley. Winston and
Clementine gaze admiringly at Ming.
Winston was fascinated by this
delectable animal, and remarked that
it satisfied the 'world's need for
cuddlability'!
A feature of life at Chartwell in 1939
was a pair of enchanting fox cubs.
Clementine is here seen with one of
them. They were called Charles-
James and Victoria. With the coming
of the war and the realization that I
was going to be away from Chartwell,
we managed to return them by
degrees to their life in the wild.

234

On 10 May 1939 Winston Churchill received a visit from Léon Blum, the French Socialist statesman and former Prime Minister. One year from that day Churchill was to become Prime Minister of Great Britain. In 1940 Léon Blum was arrested and imprisoned in France for his stout opposition to Laval and the Vichy Government: later he was transferred to Buchenwald in Germany. He survived, however, and after 1945 returned to an active political life.

235

During the earlier months of 1939, Winston was busy making additions and improvements to a cottage at the bottom of Chartwell garden; he did a great deal of the work himself.
It was intended to be a retreat for Clementine and himself in the event of war.
Here he is busily helping to tile the roof. During the first year of the war they did spend a few fleeting week-ends here, but presently Chartwell was put 'out of bounds' for security reasons.

War again

236

These next pages carry us from the last months of uneasy peace, to the outbreak of war, and through five years which saw the second world conflict in this tormented century. In personal terms this period saw Winston Churchill transformed in the public's mind from a controversial political figure into the revered leader of a nation united in a struggle – not only for our own country's survival, but for the future of civilization as we understand it. After the fall of France, when Britain stood alone for a year, the eyes of the world were fixed on our small, embattled island. In a letter to Churchill in the autumn of 1940, President Roosevelt transcribed this verse of Longfellow:

> '. . . Sail on, O Ship of State!
> Sail on, O Union, strong and great!
> Humanity with all its fears,
> With all the hopes of future years,
> Is hanging breathless on thy fate!'

Those years have left an indelible mark on the generation which lived through them. The terrors, anxieties and griefs of war are mingled with the camaraderie which the sharing of such experiences brings. These pages will perhaps remind us too, how – even when the world is crashing round one's ears – the normal events of family life retain their special place and significance.

"BRING HIM BACK—IT'S YOUR LAST CHANCE"

Events moved fast in the spring and summer of 1939. The Munich Agreement was finally in tatters when, in mid-March, Hitler annexed what was left of independent Czechoslovakia: one week later German forces took Memel from Lithuania. Great Britain and France pledged themselves to support Poland in the event of an attack by Germany. On 7 April Italy annexed Albania.
In May, Hitler and Mussolini signed a Ten Year Alliance.
Meanwhile, back at home, public awareness of the imminent danger of war was growing with every day. In the summer, a campaign for a national government gained momentum. Posters on hoardings, cartoons such as this one, and placards demanded that 'Churchill must come back'.

Holiday-time came – most people took what was to be their last carefree holiday for many long, hard years. Winston went to France in mid-August to tour the Maginot Line, afterwards joining Clementine and Mary for an agreeable painting holiday at Consuelo (Marlborough) and Jacques Balsan's beautiful home near Dreux. On 23 August the world was galvanized by the announcement that Germany and Russia had signed a non-aggression pact: Germany was now safe on her eastern borders and the message was brutally clear. Churchill returned home at once.

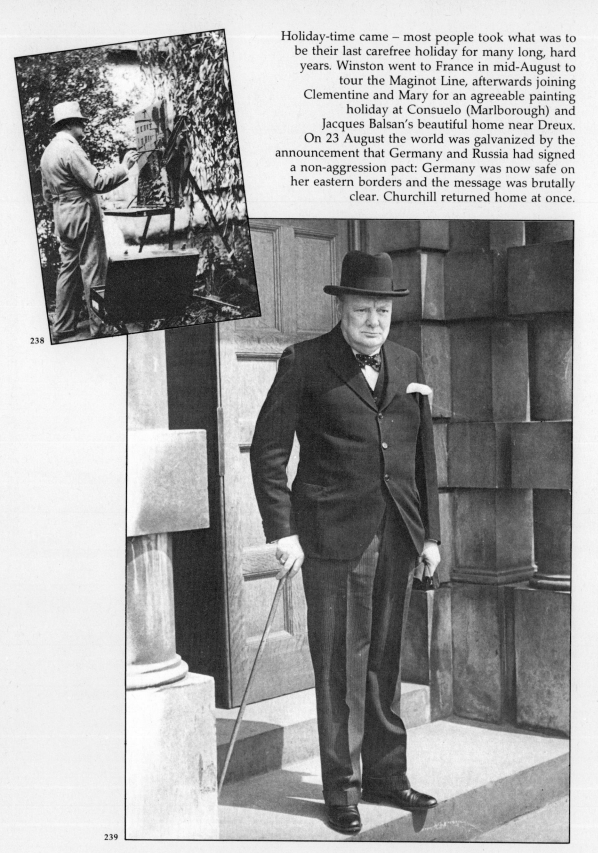

238

239

On 2 September 1939, Germany fell upon Poland. Three days later, honouring their pledge to Poland, France and Great Britain declared war on Germany. On the evening of 3 September, the Prime Minister, Neville Chamberlain, invited Winston Churchill to become First Lord of the Admiralty. Here is Winston arriving at the Admiralty on 4 September to take up his duties. Nearly a quarter of a century earlier he had left this building on relinquishing office in the bitter aftermath of the failure of the Dardanelles.
Now the Admiralty signalled the Fleet: 'Winston is back!'.

Randolph, now twenty-eight, was serving in his father's old regiment, the 4th Hussars. In late September he became engaged to Pamela Digby (then aged nineteen) the elder daughter of Lord and Lady Digby. Since Randolph's regiment might be ordered abroad at any time, the marriage took place soon afterwards in October. Here they are leaving St John's, Smith Square: the Guard of Honour was formed by Randolph's brother officers.

241

As 1939 drew to its close, the news from the war at sea was a tale of disaster and frustration. Then, with dramatic suddenness, came the Battle of the River Plate in December, which gripped and thrilled the nation. The German pocket-battleship *Graf Spee* scuttled herself in the estuary of the River Plate (between Uruguay and Argentina) after being fiercely engaged by three of our cruisers (two British, the *Ajax* and *Exeter*, and one from New Zealand, the *Achilles*). In mid-February 1940 there was a parade, inspected by the King, followed by a march of the victorious crews of *Ajax* and *Exeter* through London to the Guildhall (*Achilles* had returned to New Zealand). This flash of victory warmed the cockles of all our hearts in a long, dreary winter.

The parade was mustered on Horse Guards Parade, and the King and Queen met not only the officers and men of the ships, but also many of the relations of the men lost in the battle.

Here the Prime Minister, Neville Chamberlain, bows to the Queen, watched by the King and Churchill.

242

243

Under wartime conditions, there was
no question of living in the whole of
Admiralty House. Very quickly, the
top two floors (formerly the nurseries
and attics) were arranged as a
delightful 'maisonette', looking out over
Horse Guards Parade. Here is Clementine
at her desk soon after they moved in. This room had been the
day-nursery for John Julius Cooper (now Lord Norwich) when Duff Cooper
had been First Lord a year or two earlier; the same curtains, with their lively motif
of red and blue seahorses, did very well for the Churchills' drawing-room.
One of Clementine's activities as wife of the First Lord was to help organize
comforts for the men serving in minesweepers and other small coastal craft. Friends
and relations were harnessed to the task of knitting great jerseys and seaboot
stockings, in thick oily wool. A sample pair of stockings is on Clementine's desk.
Throughout the war, notwithstanding many other obligations, Clementine was a
conscientious member of the committee which ran a maternity home for the wives
of officers at Fulmer Chase, near Gerrards Cross. She loved her involvement in the
domestic details of running the home, and was a frequent visitor. Many of the young
wives had no homes of their own; many husbands were serving abroad; some of the
young mothers were already widows. Here is a group of mothers with their offspring.

244

Clementine launched the aircraft carrier HMS *Indomitable* at Barrow-in-Furness on 25 March 1940.
Winston and some of the family went with her. Here we all are, waiting for the great moment.
Left to right: Clementine; Winston; Mary; (?); Pamela Churchill; (?); the Third Sea Lord, Rear-
Admiral Fraser; Randolph; and, behind Randolph, Commander C.R. (Tommy) Thompson, Flag
Officer to Winston as First Lord, who remained with him throughout the war as personal assistant.

245

The pilot who would weather the storm . . . This photograph was taken a week before
Churchill became Prime Minister: he was
visiting a northern port where he went aboard a destroyer which put out to sea.

246

Since the beginning of the war in September 1939 an uneasy period of watchful inaction – except at
sea – had earned those months the title of the 'phoney war', or the 'twilight war'. But these days of
little action were fast running out. On 9 April 1940 Germany attacked Denmark and Norway
simultaneously. Denmark was overrun quickly, but the Norwegians struggled heroically with their
invaders, and called on Great Britain for help. Naval and military forces were sent with all speed, but
the campaign in Norway was a disaster (the years of lack of preparation now extorted bitter tribute).
In less than three weeks the greater number of British troops had been evacuated, a small force
remaining to endeavour, unsuccessfully (and against heavy odds), to capture the port of Narvik.
In the subsequent debate in the House of Commons on the Norwegian operations, many Members
who had hitherto supported the Government now turned angrily against the Prime Minister and his
colleagues; the resulting division saw the Government's majority crash from 240 to 81.
Mr Chamberlain, faced with open revolt in his own party and mounting indignation in the country,
now started to explore the possibility of forming a national administration. As the consultations
proceeded, it became apparent that the Labour and Liberal Parties would only serve in a government
under a new Prime Minister – and that the only man at this moment of crisis who could
command confidence was Churchill.
But further deliberations were cut short: on the night of 9–10 May, Germany invaded Holland
and Belgium. On the evening of 10 May, Mr Chamberlain resigned.
The King sent for Winston Churchill.

News Chronicle

No. 29,355   ONE PENNY   WEDNESDAY, JUNE 5, 1940   RADIO, PAGE 7

"We shall defend our island whatever the cost may be. We shall fight on the beaches, we shall fight on the landing grounds, in the fields, in the streets and in the hills. We shall never surrender."—Mr. Churchill

335,000 MEN EVACUATED

Dunkirk at Last Abandoned : The Withdrawal Complete

LAST night the French Admiralty and the British War Office announced that Dunkirk has now been abandoned to the Allies after . . . remarkable . . .

247

On 14 May 1940, German forces pierced the French defences at Sedan, quickly making a gap through which poured the Panzer divisions. Less than five days after this breakthrough, the Germans reached the coast, cutting off the Allied armies in Flanders. On 28 May the Belgians surrendered, leaving the British flank exposed. The British and allied troops fell back, fighting fiercely all the way to the Dunkirk beaches, where – cruelly exposed to low-level air attack – they awaited embarkation back to Britain. The 'miracle' of Dunkirk was now performed – the greater part of our expeditionary force and many allied troops being ferried home, by an 'armada' of ships and craft ranging from destroyers to fishing boats, across the Channel which remained blessedly calm.

Sunday Dispatch

139th Year. No. 7,234.   JUNE 23, 1940.   Radio Page 9.

TWOPENCE.

FRENCH SIGN ARMISTICE

British Government's Grief And Amazement

Hitler's Plan For . . .

Churchill Appeals To Frenchmen: 'Fight On'

THE FRENCH PLENIPOTENTIARIES SIGNED AN ARMISTICE WITH GERMANY AT 5.30 LAST NIGHT AT COMPIEGNE, FRA . . . . . . ICE WAS

NAZIS BOMB US AGAIN

Scharnhorst Torpedoed

SCHARNHORST, 26,000-TONS CRACK GERMAN BATTLE-CRUISER, HAS BEEN TORPEDOED AND BOMBED OFF TRONDHEIM, NORWAY. SHE SU . . . CONSIDERABLE DAMAGE." . . . a Nazi destroyer . . .

248

'. . . the Battle of France is over. I expect that the Battle of Britain is about to begin. Upon this battle depends the survival of Christian civilization. Upon it depends our own British life, and the long continuity of our institutions and our Empire. The whole fury and might of the enemy must very soon be turned on us.' Thus – Winston Churchill to the nation.

Here is General Charles de Gaulle, who, refusing to accept his country's defeat, came to England in the last days of the fall of France, and in a broadcast called upon his countrymen to join him in carrying on the fight with France's allies. A brilliant, dour, and difficult man – yet he came to represent the resurgent spirit of France, and became the focus for many thousands of French men and women, who, aghast at their country's capitulation, rallied to de Gaulle's clarion call, and made their ways by brave and devious means to join the Free French Forces in Britain, and later in North Africa.

249

250   251

We did not have long to wait before Hitler's 'fury and might' were turned upon us: on 10 July, the German air force began a series of formidable and almost continuous raids on the southern counties of Britain, in an attempt to gain control of the air before launching the long-planned German invasion of these islands. The attempt failed – and the Battle of Britain, and the bravery of the few hundred pilots who fought it, have passed into history. Of these pilots Winston Churchill was to say: 'Never in the field of human conflict was so much owed by so many to so few'.

Cecil Beaton took this photograph of Winston working in the Cabinet Room, September 1940.

253

Although there was much serious business to hold him in London, Winston used nevertheless to get out and around as much as possible: he wanted to 'see for himself'.
At the end of July he visited Dover and Ramsgate, which were taking a lot of punishment. He saw air-raid damage, and met A.R.P. (Air Raid Precautions) workers. Raid warnings were in force throughout his visit, and he saw two aircraft shot down in the sea not far from him. Here he is seen leaving a small hotel in Ramsgate which had been 'blitzed' a short while before his visit. (Please note the price for Bed and Breakfast!)

254

Chequers, a large Elizabethan house near Aylesbury in Buckinghamshire, is the country home of the Prime Minister of the day. It was a gift to the nation for this purpose from Lord and Lady Lee of Fareham in 1917. It was not only a princely gift – it was an imaginative one. Chequers serves equally well as a secluded retreat from the strains and hurly-burly of public life for the Prime Minister and his or her family, and as a place where foreign visitors and colleagues can be received and entertained in agreeable, beautiful and relaxing surroundings. Previous Prime Ministers had used Chequers – as was the main intention of the donors – as a place of retreat and repose, but during Churchill's wartime tenure it became an extension of his No. 10 machine: business and the war could be conducted round the clock as well from there as from London. Secretaries, telephone operators and despatch riders were all accommodated. An agreeable change from city life it most certainly was, but it was hardly a place of rest (for Clementine at least, and despite an efficient staff):visitors succeeded each other in veritable 'shifts' over the weekends – foreign guests, government colleagues, service chiefs and so on. However, the house is large, and members of the family could nearly always be fitted in.

255

256

The difficulty of finding suitable domestic staff in wartime, and the necessity for strict security, led to the decision being taken to staff Chequers with volunteers from the women's services, and this very sensible solution holds good to this day. The picture above shows the Great Hall, circa 1940.

Winston and his family, however, did sometimes relax at Chequers: these family snapshots were taken during the summer of 1940, when invasion threatened – they are somehow rather reassuring in their normality.

Above right: Pamela Churchill. She was expecting a child – a son, born at Chequers on 10 October 1940: 'little' Winston.

Below: Clementine with Jock (now Sir John) Colville: he was in the Prime Minister's Private Office except for his period of service as a pilot in the R.A.F.V.R. He and later his wife became very close friends of both Winston and Clementine and their family.

258

Above: Diana and Duncan Sandys' two elder children, Julian, born in 1936, and Edwina, born in 1938.

Before the "Blitz" at Downing Street Love and Christmas wishes from Clemmie

Cecil Beaton took this charming photograph of Clementine at tea-time in the drawing-room at
10 Downing Street, just before the 'Blitz' on London started in September 1940. Soon No. 10
was to become too dangerous to work or sleep in, and other arrangements were made. But in this
picture the summer sunshine streams in on what might be a peacetime example of 'gracious living'.
The large portrait of Winston is the Orpen, painted in 1915.

On 13 September 1940, a stick of bombs from a lone dive-bomber fell on **Buckingham Palace** and its garden. The King and Queen had just arrived from Windsor, and from a sitting-room overlooking the Quadrangle they saw two of the bombs fall about eighty yards away. It was not known for a long time just how close they had been to mortal danger that morning.
This picture of the King and Queen showing their Prime Minister the extensive damage to their home had a marvellous 'tonic' effect on morale . . . 'We're all in this together.'

262

This is one of the best-known – and certainly for their family one of the best-loved – photographs of Winston and Clementine. It tells one so much about the closeness of their relationship: their natural and spontaneous affection; the earnest discussion of tidings and events whether good or bad. Winston told Clementine everything: he trusted her completely. In this instance, one can see they are in sombre mood. The picture was taken at the end of September 1940, when London was in the grip of the 'Blitz', and the City and East End had been heavily bombed. Winston always wanted to visit the scenes of devastation, and to see for himself the rescue operations in progress; owing to a large number of unexploded bombs, it was, on this occasion, impracticable to go to the City by road. Winston therefore went down river by launch to inspect the recently bombed areas, and Clementine went with him.

263

Bombing raids caused anxiety to those in charge of the Prime Minister's security, and his 'regular as clockwork' weekends at Chequers were thought to be a risk, and the place itself easily identifiable from the air. It was thought prudent, therefore, to find an alternative weekend retreat for him. At this point, Mr and Mrs Ronald Tree offered to shelter Winston, his family and staff at their beautiful and historic home Ditchley, in Oxfordshire (above). Both Ronnie and Nancy Tree were half-American by birth; he had been brought up here, and both made England their home. As a Conservative Member of Parliament, Ronnie Tree had from the early days supported Winston in his fight for re-armament. Their generous offer of hospitality solved the weekend problem, and it became customary that when the moon was high, the Churchills and their entourage would repair to Ditchley instead of Chequers. Winston and Clementine, of course, already knew the Trees, and the group on the right was taken during a summer weekend in 1937. Top steps: Nancy and Ronnie Tree; Malcolm Bullock, M.P.; Earl of Erne; Anthony Eden, M.P. Second step: Countess of Erne; Viscountess Gage: (half-hidden) Beatrice Eden and (below her) Priscilla Bullock. Bottom step: Clementine and Winston. Back to camera: Viscount Gage.

265   266

On the outbreak of war Diana sent her two small children to live in one of the cottages at Chartwell and to be cared for by 'Nana' Whyte. She herself joined the Women's Royal Naval Service (W.R.N.S.) and was commissioned as a Second Officer. Later, when Julian and Edwina returned from the country, she left the W.R.N.S. to look after them; shortly afterwards, in 1941, Duncan was invalided out of the army following a very serious motor accident.

Duncan Sandys was an officer in the Territorial Army (51st Anti-Aircraft Regiment). He went to Norway with his battery, which was one of the last units to leave in the final evacuation. Thereafter he was engaged on experimental anti-aircraft work until the accident which terminated his army career. He had been a Member of Parliament since 1935. After two junior posts, Duncan became Minister of Works in 1944–45, the first of several high Ministerial offices he was to hold.

267

Randolph, who had gone to North Africa with his regiment, returned to England for a time during the autumn and winter of 1940. At the end of September he was returned unopposed at a by-election as Conservative Unionist Member of Parliament for Preston (Lancashire). His time in England happily coincided with the birth of his son. Back in North Africa, Randolph became a General Staff Officer at G.H.Q., Middle East (Cairo). This snapshot of him was taken in 1941. He later joined the Special Air Service, and took part in some dangerous and dashing operations.

268   269

During the first two years of the war, Sarah and Vic Oliver were busy with their stage careers, acting sometimes together and sometimes apart. But, sadly, difficulties began to beset their marriage, and in 1941 they separated, and Vic (he was an American citizen) went back to the United States; they were not actually divorced until some years later. Sarah joined the Women's Auxiliary Air Force (W.A.A.F.) in October 1941, as an Aircraftwoman (Second class). After her initial training at Morecambe (where this photograph of her was taken), Sarah was trained in photographic interpretation of aerial photographs – highly technical and top secret work. She was subsequently commissioned, and spent the rest of the war doing this intelligence work.
Above, Aircraftwoman (Second class) Oliver newly equipped with her kit.

Just before I was eighteen, in September 1941, I and my cousin and great friend Judy Montagu enlisted in the women's Auxiliary Territorial Service (A.T.S.): we both wanted to join the Mixed (men/women) Anti-Aircraft Batteries which were being formed. We underwent our technical training at Oswestry in Shropshire, and both attained the dazzling rank of Local/Acting/Lance-Corporals! After our period of training, we were both posted to a Heavy Mixed Anti-Aircraft Battery at Enfield, Middlesex.

270

In the summer of 1941, our family was saddened by the death of Jack's wife, Goonie Churchill.
She was fifty-six, and had been ill with cancer. Her death brought back, for Clementine
particularly, memories of the First World War – when they had shared nurseries and houses and
seaside holidays, and of how Goonie had been her great confidante and comforter in the
dark days after the Dardanelles.
In this picture, taken in 1937, Goonie is with her only daughter, Clarissa (then aged seventeen).

271

Averell Harriman, here photographed at Ditchley, was one of the remarkable Americans
whom the President was to send out on vital assignments. In 1940 Harriman came to London to
pioneer the arrangements for Lend-Lease, which were to be formalized the following year, and
of which he became the principal administrator. In 1941 he was in charge of the American
mission to Moscow, and in 1943 was appointed Ambassador to the U.S.S.R. Urbane, clever, calm
and dedicated, his contribution to both his country and our own was outstanding.

Early in 1941, there came to Britain two Americans whose importance to Anglo-American friendship and understanding it would be difficult to over-estimate: Harry Hopkins, and John Gilbert Winant. Harry Hopkins was President Roosevelt's closest confidant, and he came on his first visit to Britain in January 1941 as the President's personal envoy. He at once established a close and frank dialogue with Winston. Despite the frailty of his health, Hopkins was to be in the ensuing years (both during visits to this country and in Washington at the President's side), a strong and sensitive link between Roosevelt and Churchill.

In February 1941, John Gilbert Winant took up his appointment as United States Ambassador to Great Britain. He soon formed close relationships with many of our wartime leaders, and especially with Churchill. But he also made a mark in the country as a whole because of his understanding of our problems, his sharing of our dangers and difficulties, and his championship of our needs. On the personal side, 'Gil' became a close family friend.

In this photograph, taken in 1942 during a river trip, are (left to right): W.S.C.; Harry Hopkins; John Gilbert Winant; William C. Bullitt; and the First Lord of the Admiralty, A.V. Alexander.

No account of the war in Britain – not even a personal record such as this one – would be complete without some mention of the weaponry of words employed by Winston Churchill in his role as Britain's war leader. It was said: 'He mobilized the English language and sent it to war'. Whether the words were addressed to the House of Commons (in open or secret session), whether they were brief impromptu speeches made, perhaps from a pile of rubble, to rescue workers and bystanders in the aftermath of a bombing raid, or whether they were in the form of his regular broadcast addresses to the nation, Churchill's wartime speeches formed a strong, gleaming thread in the fabric of the nation's morale, endurance and determination.

273

274

Listening intently to one of Churchill's broadcasts are some customers in the Green Dragon pub at Flaunden, Herts . . .

When Churchill broadcast, people gathered round the radio to listen, whether they were in pubs, factories, offices or clubs, or even in the street, pausing to listen through an open window.

It was not all oratory – although there were some stirring passages which may perhaps endure as long as men love freedom. There were hard, bald facts; there were jokes – grim, 'Yes, I don't think' sort of jokes (much appreciated by the Cockneys in particular). There were warnings of perils and hardships ahead; and there was always a reminder that this was no mere conflict for personal survival alone but that we all served a higher purpose. And there was always the profound, unshakeable belief that, despite all difficulties, griefs and dangers, victory would be ours in the end.

Churchill always seemed to call (with unerring touch) upon those deep reserves of feeling that people never know they possess until some great trial is thrust upon them: emotional responses which the British, in particular, bury deep. All these Churchill called forth – these he expressed for a whole nation. The broadcasts and speeches were mostly addressed to his own countrymen, but others listened also: America listened, growing increasingly sympathetic to our cause, and increasingly aware that it was their cause, too. And now we know that millions of people in the occupied countries listened – at great peril – and drew from those broadcasts strength and hope in the long night of their imprisonment.

.. and a family in London's East End.

It was very soon realized that 10 Downing Street as a building was unsafe, and even after the garden-level rooms had been shored-up and fortified so that 'business as usual' could be carried on despite air raids, the arrangements were not adequate or safe for the number of people who lived and worked in the building. But underneath the modern stone government office building at Storey's Gate (at the Whitehall end of Birdcage Walk) there had already been constructed a complete subterranean complex of offices and shelters from which the War Cabinet and Chiefs of Staff could operate and in which they could live under conditions of heavy bombing. This was admirable for daily work and for a 'last redoubt' situation, but was not suitable for day-to-day living. The problem was solved by the conversion of a series of offices on the first floor of the Storey's Gate building, immediately over the underground War Rooms, into a flat for Winston and Clementine and their personal staff. The work was done with the utmost haste and with as little expense as possible: one can see in the pictures that

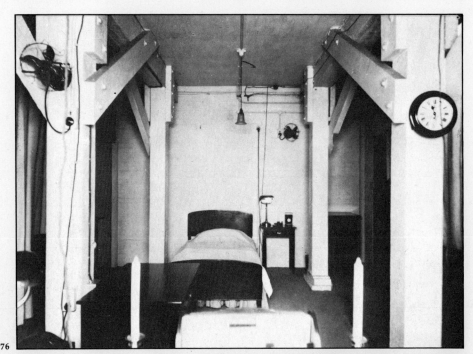

276

277

The Prime Minister's sleeping arrangements (top) in the underground
War Room complex and (above) the sitting-room in the 'Annexe' flat.

the pipes running through the rooms at ceiling height were not cased in, and the office overhead-lights remained. The windows, deep set in the solid walls of the building, were fitted with thick steel shutters, which were closed during air raids. Clementine had the rooms painted in delicate colours, and she brought some of their own furniture, pictures and other belongings to mix with the 'government issue': the gaunt, unprepossessing rooms really looked quite pretty. Winston always preferred, whenever possible, to hold Cabinet meetings in the Cabinet Room at No. 10, and to receive and entertain his and Clementine's guests over there as well – merely using the 'Annexe' (as the new apartments came to be called) as sleeping quarters for themselves and their staff. But presently this became difficult administratively, and unwise from a safety point of view, and so Winston and Clementine came more and more to conduct their whole life from the 'Annexe'.

278

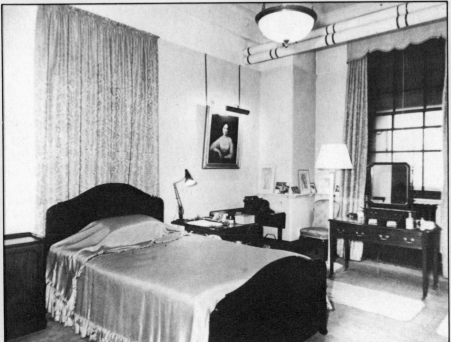

279

Clementine's bedroom (top) and Winston's bedroom (above). The portrait is of his American grandmother, Clara Hall Jerome.

On 4 August 1941, Winston Churchill sailed in the battleship *Prince of Wales* for Placentia Bay, Newfoundland, where he had a rendezvous with President Roosevelt. The two leaders had corresponded from the early days of the war – now they met in this lonely bay to confer on many matters, and to cement a friendship which was to be of vital importance not only to Anglo-American understanding, but to the whole free world. The secrecy surrounding this Atlantic Charter meeting was complete: the U.S. newspapers announced that the President had left 'for a fishing trip' – hence this delightful cartoon by Low.

Under the shadow of the great guns, the ships' companies of the USS *Augusta* (seen in background) and HMS *Prince of Wales* gather with their leaders for Sunday morning service. Now this picture strikes a tragic note, for some months later the *Prince of Wales* was sunk by the Japanese off the coast of Malaya with grievous loss of life.

On the night of 10 August, the President invited Winston and his colleagues to dine with him on the *Augusta*. Here is the menu card signed by some of those present.

284

In January 1941, Winston paid a visit with General Sikorski to units of the Polish army stationed and training in Scotland. It must have been bitter weather – some gallant Pole has lent Clementine his greatcoat. General Sikorski is on the right. The little girl in the picture below must be in her forties now. I wonder if she remembers asking a gentleman in a stove-pipe hat and a macintosh for his autograph, one wintry day at a railway station?

285

286

'Vive la France!': watched by Clementine, Winston raises his glass in the garden of No. 10 to five French boys aged between sixteen and twenty, who had escaped from the Brittany coast in two canoes. Fired on by German troops when they were only a few yards from the shore, they had nevertheless made their escape under cover of darkness. It took them thirty-six hours to reach the English coast, where they were tossed up on the beach in a cold and exhausted condition.

287

It is customary for Sovereign and Prime Minister to have a regular weekly talk about the affairs of the nation, and every Tuesday Winston was received in audience by the King. During these years there grew up between the King and his Prime Minister a more than usually close relationship, and very often after the official audience was over Winston would be invited to stay on and lunch at Buckingham Palace; frequently the Queen would be there as well. So that their conversation could range over many matters it became usual for the servants to withdraw, and the King and Queen and Winston would help themselves.

On the occasion when this picture was taken, Their Majesties had been to luncheon with Winston and Clementine at No. 10, and Winston is taking leave of them on the doorstep.

On 12 April 1941, Churchill as Chancellor of Bristol University conferred the Honorary Degree of Doctor of Laws on Mr Winant (American Ambassador) and Mr Menzies (Prime Minister of Australia). During the preceding night Bristol had been heavily bombed: nevertheless the ceremony took place. Later Gil Winant described it in his own words: 'The company were in academic robes, as is customary, but under them they wore a most extraordinary assortment of clothes. Some were in Service uniform, others in Civil Defence uniform, many in fireman's dress, and nearly all still soaked from their labors. They had been hard at it all night but all turned up ... The age-old ceremony went on against a new background. Through the windows we saw the smoke and flame and hoses of the firemen still playing on the burning buildings next to the University. And now and then we heard the crump of a delayed-action bomb.'

Below left, Winston with Mr Menzies (left) and Mr Winant after the degree ceremony.

289

Later the same day, Churchill and his guests visited the areas of Bristol worst hit by the raid: everywhere people came running to greet him. Above right, Winston is talking to a woman who had just been extricated from the ruins of her home.

290

This charming photograph shows Winston with the members of his Private Office in 1941. They were a wonderful team: several of them were to go on to brilliant careers; they were also true and trusted friends, and bore the heat and burden of many a day (and night) of crisis. Left to right (front row): 'Jock' Colville; W.S.C.; John Martin; Anthony Bevir. Left to right (back row): Leslie Rowan; John Peck; Miss Watson; Commander C.R. Thompson; Charles Barker.

291

292

Some colleagues, counsellors and friends . . . Professor Lindemann ('The Prof.'), Winston's friend, philosopher and scientific 'guru' since 1925, was throughout the war his chief scientific adviser – and was in the Cabinet as Paymaster-General from 1942-5. He was created the first Baron Cherwell in 1941. Here he is (above left) hurrying to a meeting at No. 10 in 1940, with an assistant.
Brendan Bracken (above right) continued as a close associate of Winston throughout the war. From 1940-1 he was his Parliamentary Private Secretary, and he then became Minister of Information from 1941 until the end of the war. Here he is leaving No. 10 with Winston to go to the House of Commons in June 1940. Lord Beaverbrook (below), the Canadian-born proprietor of the *Daily Express*. Max Beaverbrook had been a friend of Winston's since the First World War. Their friendship had its ups and downs – but it endured. Clementine never really liked Max, although she mellowed towards him in after years: above all, she deeply mistrusted his advice and political influence over Winston and in this she was often right. Appointed Minister of Aircraft Production in 1940, Beaverbrook performed wonders, earning for himself the title of 'The Wizard of Oz'. From 1941 he held various other government posts. This picture shows him with Winston on board
HMS *Prince of Wales* at the time of the Atlantic Charter meeting with President Roosevelt.

293

On 22 June 1941 Germany invaded Russia, with whom she had signed a non-aggression pact almost exactly two years before. Churchill, although a lifelong enemy of Communism, at once pledged Britain's support as an ally against Nazi Germany. As the tidal wave of the German forces swept across the Russian frontier and into its heartland, sympathy for the sufferings of the Russian people, and admiration for the heroic defence of their country, grew daily.

For the moment there was little Britain could do to help their new ally, but from the beginning donations great and small came flooding in to the Soviet Embassy in London. At first there was no other focal point or way in which people could demonstrate their sympathy and desire to help. Soon, however, various committees were formed, mainly by left-wing organizations.

In October, the Red Cross and Order of St John started an Aid to Russia Fund, and invited Clementine Churchill to be the Chairman of the Appeal Committee. She accepted with alacrity, and from that time until 1945, when the Appeal closed, 'Mrs Churchill's Aid to Russia Fund' (for that was how it very soon came to be known) absorbed a very large part of her thought and energy. Soon this Fund eclipsed all others, both in its scope of appeal and the dimension and effectiveness of the aid it was able to send to our hard-pressed ally. Enthusiasm for the Fund was amazing: by Christmas 1941, 'Mrs Churchill's Aid to Russia Fund' had passed the £1,000,000 mark, and money was still rolling in.

294

295

Throughout the country, money-raising events great and small were organized to help the Aid to Russia Fund. The England football captain Eddie Hapgood is seen (above right) introducing Clementine to members of the team before the charity match against Scotland at Wembley in January 1942. Above left, Clementine is receiving a cheque presented to her on behalf of the people of Doncaster by the Mayor. Left to right: The Mayor of Doncaster; Clementine; the Mayoress. This picture is rather interesting because the party is having tea in the fortified downstairs rooms at No. 10, where Winston and Clementine always preferred to receive their guests, when conditions permitted. The rooms were strengthened with stanchions and beams rather like pit-props which gave something of the appearance of a ship's wardroom. The decorations were simple, and the starkness was relieved mainly by family photographs.

296

Churchill and the Soviet Ambassador Maisky deep in conversation at a luncheon at the Soviet Embassy in August 1941. Our new allies were difficult and 'prickly', and mutual blandishments were most necessary. Here, Winston seems to be giving the Ambassador a real 'old-fashioned look'.

On 7 December 1941 the Japanese made their world-shaking attack on Pearl Harbor. With America henceforward beside Britain in the struggle, the issue could no longer be in doubt. In his own words, when Churchill went to bed that night he 'slept the sleep of the saved and the thankful'. Now he felt he must see the President again as soon as possible, and he and his colleagues therefore set sail in HMS *Duke of York* on 13 December. A few days before his departure the news had been received of the sinking by the Japanese of the *Prince of Wales* and *Repulse* – a crushing blow.

I went up to Scotland with my father to see him off. The weather was wild, and dangers lurked beneath the waves. On board HMS *Duke of York*, 13 December 1941; Lance-Corporal Mary Churchill is saluted by the Prime Minister. Winston spent Christmas 1941 at the White House. During his visit many plans were made, and the friendship between Churchill and President Roosevelt, between the Chiefs of Staff and government ministers and officials of both countries – now comrades-in-arms – was further consolidated. For the first time Churchill addressed a session of Congress. From Washington he went on to Ottawa for a few days, and there also he was asked to address the Canadian Parliament.

Back at home in England, Winston continued to get around the country as much as possible visiting bombed cities, inspecting troops, training establishments, and so on. He usually travelled long distances on a special train in which he and his entourage could work, eat and sleep: the train, moreover, could be 'plugged in' at various halts to secure telephone communication. Thus on his tours (which were of immense importance to general morale, and to his own sense of what people were doing and feeling) Winston was never out of touch with events, and there was no break in the work of waging the war.

One of the worst-bombed of our cities was Plymouth and the nearby Devonport Dockyard. These areas had been severely blitzed for five successive nights in late April 1941. Winston, with Clementine, toured the city on 2 May in an open car accommpanied by Lady Astor, the Lady Mayoress, and Conservative Member of Parliament for the Sutton Division of Plymouth since 1919 (American-born, she had entered the House of Commons as the first woman to take her seat). Winston and the redoubtable Nancy had never liked each other, and had often disagreed politically, but she won his true admiration now by her courage and constant care for the people of Plymouth in their ordeal. Here they are outside the Astors' house in Plymouth. An independent observer of this tour wrote that Churchill was 'fierce faced, firmly balanced on the back of the car, with great tears of angry sorrow in his eyes'. In the lower picture, Winston is visiting blitzed Battersea.

300

301

For the Allies, 1941 and 1942 were years of almost continuous bad tidings – albeit lightened from time to time by gleams of victory, such as the hunting and sinking of the German battleship *Bismarck* in May 1941. The war in the North African desert swung to and fro. At sea the Navy reeled under the loss of capital ships, and in the Atlantic, submarines took their toll of our lifelines of food and arms from America. In the Far East the Japanese forces swept relentlessly on: Singapore surrendered, and 60,000 troops disappeared into a long and grim captivity. Thereafter the Japanese overran Burma and the Dutch East Indies, and on 1 May 1942 they took Mandalay, and the British withdrew towards India. At home in Britain, the 'Blitz' on London in the autumn and winter of 1940 (when the city was attacked by an average of 200 German bombers for 57 successive nights) had been succeeded by more spasmodic raids on the capital, and devastating air attacks on provincial cities.

Wartime life in Britain was grey and arid: food, clothes and petrol were strictly rationed and, particularly on the civilian front, daily life was a dour slog. Yet the dogged spirit of determination and endurance did not flag, and people were aware of our growing strength, and power to retaliate. The R.A.F. was penetrating deeper into Germany with bombing attacks, and the invasion armies were in training throughout the British Isles. In all these hard times Winston Churchill had indeed become the symbol of our country's resolution and endurance. In June 1942 Churchill went again to Washington to confer with the President upon the launching of the Second Front in Europe, and in August he was once more on his travels – this time to the war theatre in the Middle East, where major changes in the military command made General Alexander Commander-in-Chief Middle East, and General Bernard Montgomery commander of the Eighth Army. The three men are seen here together.

302

303

Here Winston is seen talking to a man whose counsel and friendship were equally precious to him –
Field Marshal Jan Smuts, Prime Minister of South Africa.
Throughout the war, Winston kept in close and constant touch with him.

Homeward bound via Cairo, Churchill visited the Eighth Army forward areas. Here he is with their
new G.O.C., General Montgomery (henceforth 'Monty'), who, not to be outdone by Winston,
is wearing an Australian hat! The troops gave Winston a heartwarming welcome.
On 23 October 1942, at El Alamein, the heaviest artillery barrage ever known was the preliminary to
twelve days of fierce fighting, resulting in a major victory for the Allies over
Field Marshal Rommel's army. On 8 November, United States and British forces landed on the
French North African coast. Later, Churchill wrote: 'It may almost be said,
"Before Alamein we never had a victory. After Alamein we never had a defeat".'

In October 1942, a most welcome and important visitor came to Britain – Eleanor Roosevelt, the wife
of the President and a remarkable and politically significant personality in her own right.
Mrs Roosevelt spent three weeks in this country, undertaking an exhaustive (and exhausting!) tour.
She stayed with the King and Queen at Buckingham Palace, and spent a weekend with Winston and
Clementine at Chequers: and they also gave a dinner party for her at No. 10. But most of her time
was spent in finding out just what the war meant, in terms of everyday life, to ordinary men and
women. Just before Mrs Roosevelt took her departure, Winston sent her a farewell letter:
'You certainly have left golden footprints behind you,' he wrote.

305

Above, Mrs Roosevelt with a Civil Defence official walking through a badly blitzed area
of London at Aldersgate.
Below, Mrs Roosevelt, listened to by Clementine, is here addressing ferry pilots, some of them
American, at an Air Transport Auxiliary establishment.

306

PICTURE POST

Roosevelt and Churchill at the Casablanca "Unconditional Surrender" Conference.

HULTON'S NATIONAL WEEKLY

In this issue:

CASABLANCA: PRELUDE TO ATTA

FEBRUARY 13, 1943   Vol. 18.

In 1943, Roosevelt and Churchill were to meet on four occasions; and in addition to these top-level meetings, Winston made frequent journeys to keep in touch with commanders and men 'on the spot' in various theatres of war. These journeyings not only involved elements of risk, but were, for the most part, long, tiring and uncomfortable: moreover, wherever he went, he carried the inescapable burden of the war. Winston was now in his sixty-ninth year, and in his closest circle there was some concern for his health. But none of these considerations daunted or deterred him. Churchill's first journey in 1943 was to Casablanca in North Africa, where he again met in conference with President Roosevelt.

Randolph was able to join his father at Casablanca. Behind Winston and Randolph are Commander 'Tommy' Thompson, and his detective, Inspector Thompson.

I am very glad to have found this photograph (below) of Mr Frank Sawyers – my father's faithful valet who accompanied him on all his journeyings, looking after him with devoted, nanny-like care.

Winston had been away in all five weeks; at the station to meet him on his return were colleagues as well as members of his family. Left to right (front row): Clementine; Julian Sandys (aged six); Winston; Diana Sandys. Left to right (back row): (behind Clementine) Clement Attlee (Deputy Prime Minister); Sir John Anderson (Lord President of the Council); (behind Diana) Oliver Lyttelton (Minister of Production).

PREMIER:
A LUNG INFLAMED

An official bulletin from No. 10 Downing-street last night said the Prime Minister had had a comfortable day.

There is a small area of inflammation in one lung, but the fever is lower and his general

310A   311

But these travels had taken their toll: Winston had been home less than a week when he developed pneumonia. His illness could not be kept secret, and bulletins were issued: there was considerable public anxiety. However, after a period of convalescence at Chequers, he made a good recovery. One of the doctors signing the bulletin was Sir Charles Wilson, who had become Winston's personal physician in 1940, and who was to care for him until his death. During the war, Lord Moran (as he became in 1943) accompanied Winston on nearly all his travels – most fortunately as it was to prove on several occasions.

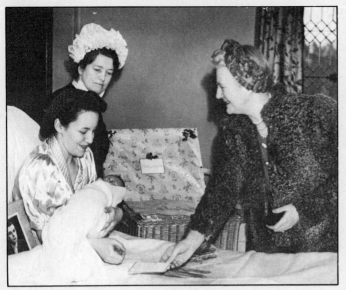

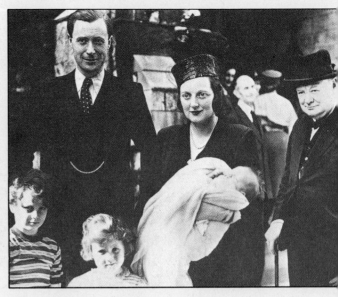

312

In January 1943, Clementine performed an informal and domestic ceremony. She presented to the mother of the *thousandth* baby to be born at the Fulmer Chase Maternity Home (of which she was a Committee member) a layette given by Queen Elizabeth. Please note the absent father's photograph on the pillow.

This snapshot also provides us with a clear view of the 'turban' arrangement worn by Clementine. Early in the war she had adopted this form of headwear, only wearing hats on very formal occasions. Modelled on the scarf-bandanas worn by thousands of factory workers and others who had to have their hair out of the way (or as a concealment for curlers!), Clementine had a veritable 'library' made in different materials, patterns and colours. Throughout long days of touring bombed cities, lunching with Lord Mayors, and inspecting canteens and hostels, her turbans were always 'just right'; they were very becoming to her, and maintained her immaculate appearance.

As with most families then, our family feasts and occasions had to be fitted in wherever our war-governed lives allowed. In the summer of 1943, Diana gave birth to her third and last child, Celia. Here is a christening picture, outside the chapel in the Crypt of the House of Commons. Left to right: Duncan, Diana with baby Celia, Winston; in front: Julian and Edwina Sandys.

314

On 13 May 1943 General Alexander had signalled the Prime Minister: 'Sir: It is my duty to report that the Tunisian Campaign is over. All enemy resistance has ceased. We are masters of the North African shores.' This was a tremendous milestone on our dusty way. We knew we had many an ordeal still to weather, but we were now *sure* of victory. The City of London conferred upon Winston the Freedom of the City, and it seemed like a celebration for the great North African victory and the turning of the tide. Sarah and I accompanied our parents on 30 June to the Guildhall for the 'Freedom' ceremony.

In May 1943, Winston was again in Washington for talks with the President; he went by sea in the *Queen Mary* (the great passenger liner which had been converted into a troopship), but returned to England by air, flying via Gibraltar and Algiers, where he paused for talks with General Eisenhower and other commanders. This photograph was taken in early June at General Eisenhower's headquarters in Algiers. It is a remarkable picture because gathered around Churchill are so many of the men upon whom depended – whether as commanders in the field, or as politicians or strategists – the waging of the war. It also demonstrates the closeness of Anglo-American co-operation: most of the commands were now integrated.

Left to right: Anthony Eden (Foreign Secretary); General Sir Alan Brooke (Chief of the Imperial General Staff); Air Chief Marshal Sir Arthur Tedder (Allied Air Commander in the Mediterranean); Admiral of the Fleet Sir Andrew Cunningham (Allied Naval Commander-in-Chief in the Mediterranean); General Sir Harold Alexander (Deputy Supreme Allied Commander in North Africa); General George Marshall (one of the most outstanding American generals and administrators, and after the war famous as the moving spirit behind the life-saving Marshall Plan, upon which the reconstruction of Europe so heavily depended. At this time he was Chairman of the Joint Chiefs of Staff Committee); General Eisenhower (Supreme Allied Commander in North Africa); General Sir Bernard Montgomery (Commander of the Eighth Army).

316

The next full-blown conference took place at Quebec in September 1943. There was much to discuss: the war in the Far East; the invasion of Italy (which was imminent, and took place on 3 September); and now, growing ever nearer, 'Operation Overlord' – the invasion of Europe.

The principals in this meeting were the President, Mr Mackenzie King (Prime Minister of Canada) and Winston Churchill. Accompanying Winston on this occasion were Clementine and myself (now a commissioned officer) as A.D.C. Before the start of the conference, the President invited Winston and some of his party to spend a few days at his home at Hyde Park, on the shores of the Hudson River. This was a most enjoyable interlude. When the train arrived at the riverside station, the President himself was there to drive Winston to the house.

F.D.R., despite his crippling disability, was amazingly active and independent. Here he is driving Winston, with Brendan Bracken (nearest to the camera) and Tommy Thompson in the back.

317

Returned to Quebec, the conference got under way. The Governor-General of Canada, the Earl of Athlone (Queen Mary's brother), and Princess Alice, Countess of Athlone (a granddaughter of Queen Victoria), came from Ottawa to greet the President and the other overseas guests.

Winston and his party lived in the Citadel (a royal residence, and made available by courtesy of the King). It is a fortress castle, crowning the cliffs above the St Lawrence river and overlooking the city of Quebec. The picture above was taken from the terrace, just after the President had arrived.

Left to right (back row): Lord Athlone; Prime Minister Mackenzie King; Sir Alexander Harding (Permanent Under Secretary at the Foreign Office); Brendan Bracken (Minister of Information).

Left to right (front row): Anthony Eden (Foreign Secretary); the President; Princess Alice (wife of the Governor-General); Winston Churchill.

After the conference, Winston and Clementine took a few days holiday, staying
with Colonel Frank Clarke at his fishing lodge on the shores of
Lac des Neiges in the Laurentian Mountains. Winston (new to trout fishing)
tried his luck. Here he is (above left), precariously balanced in a canoe – he
caught one or two fish, much to his delight. Above right, he and Clementine
enjoy some peace, and the autumn sunshine.

320

After the Quebec Conference was over, Winston and his entourage went to Washington for further
consultations. My father, my mother and I were staying at the White House as guests of the
Roosevelts. While we were there, the news was received that Italy had surrendered unconditionally
on 7 September. Victory seemed a stride nearer. We all embarked for home in HMS *Renown*,
which was awaiting the party at Halifax. Here is Winston waving farewell to crowds gathered on the
quayside at Halifax. I am with him, and the ship's captain.

1943 might well have been called 'The Year of Conferences'! Almost exactly two months after his return from Quebec and Washington, Winston was off again on his travels. His principal destination was Teheran, the capital of Persia (now Iran), where the first joint meeting of the 'Big Three' – Roosevelt–Stalin–Churchill – had been arranged. But before keeping that important rendezvous, Churchill had some other calls to make. The party embarked once more in HMS *Renown* on 12 November and, passing through the Straits of Gibraltar, called in on Algiers, arriving in Malta on 17 November. Here Winston met Generals Eisenhower and Alexander. It should be mentioned that from the start of the journey Winston had been suffering from a heavy cold and sore throat (further aggravated by various innoculations administered before his departure from England). During the voyage he remained most of the time in his cabin, although he continued to work on papers. Sarah (now Section Officer Oliver, W.A.A.F.) went with him this time as his A.D.C. (In view of general anxieties about Winston's health, the War Cabinet had expressed a wish that a member of his family should always accompany him on his travels.) Despite being quite unwell, Winston nevertheless attended a formal dinner given by the Governor of Malta, and toured the bombarded and battered dockyard where he received a tumultuous welcome. Churchill and his party disembarked at Alexandria on 21 November and, staying in a villa close by the Pyramids, conferred for the next six days with the President and the Chinese leader Generalissimo Chiang Kai-shek. Far Eastern affairs dominated the discussions. These talks over, Roosevelt and Churchill, with their large attendant staffs, flew on to Teheran to meet with Stalin.

321

Here is Winston on board *Renown* en route for Alexandria. Left to right: A.D.C., Sarah; W.S.C.; Admiral Sir Andrew Cunningham (then First Sea Lord); behind him, Major Desmond Morton (a longtime friend and supplier of information to Winston in pre-war days, now on the Prime Minister's personal staff and his liaison with the intelligence services); Lord Moran, Winston's doctor.

The three-day meeting at Teheran was indeed momentous, but it was not without its difficulties and tensions, and for Winston, these were made more onerous by the fact that he had not really recovered from the indisposition which had dogged him right from the start of his journey. However, despite any differences between them, all was friendship and cheer on the evening of 30 November – Winston's sixty-ninth birthday. The President and Stalin dined as Winston's guests at the British Legation. Here, Winston admires his birthday cake.

At the Big Three Conference.
The A.D.C. meets the President!
Front row: Marshal Stalin; President Roosevelt (talking to Section Officer Oliver); Winston Churchill.
Behind: Mr Molotov (Soviet Commissar for Foreign Affairs); Averell Harriman (U.S.A. Ambassador to Moscow); Sir Archibald Clark-Kerr (British Ambassador to Moscow); Anthony Eden (British Secretary of State for Foreign Affairs).

But it was not yet time for Winston to turn homeward: from Teheran he headed back to Cairo, where he was able again to have private talks with President Roosevelt. Many vital and painful decisions had to be taken at this period on the priorities to be accorded to the various projected operations in both western and eastern hemispheres: it was impossible to aid one without weakening another; the succession of consultations was therefore absolutely necessary. While in Cairo, Winston paid a visit to his old regiment, the 4th Hussars (he was their Colonel-in-Chief): he received a rousing welcome from these seasoned soldiers.

" GOD REST-YOU MERRY, GENTLEMAN, LET NOTHING YOU DISMAY

During this return visit to Cairo it was clear that Winston was extremely exhausted. Lord Moran and others did their utmost to persuade him to head straight for home, instead of carrying out his plan to go via Tunis to see General Eisenhower, and then to fly on to the Italian war front. But nothing would dissuade Winston, so the party set out for Tunis on 11 December. But on his arrival there, Winston had to admit that he was completely at the end of his tether. Fortunately, Eisenhower had a villa nearby at Carthage, which he most hospitably placed at Winston's disposal. Lord Moran, realising that this was no passing indisposition, sent for a specialist and nurses: pneumonia was diagnosed. Clementine flew out to be with him: her own journey – a night flight in an unheated Liberator – was quite an adventure. Her arrival had a tonic effect.

Anxiety for the patient was not confined to his family and friends: everyone from the King and Queen and Parliament, to men and women in the streets, expressed their anxiety and solicitude. Soon Winston began to improve, and on Christmas Day he had his first meal outside his bedroom.

A few days before the end of the old year – 1943 – the whole party flew to Marrakech, where Winston was to spend his convalescence. Although (contrary to the doctors' wishes) Winston had scarcely missed a day when he did not see papers or attempt some work, he had been very ill, and it took him some little while to regain his habitual strength. But he determinedly kept himself in contact with and in control of events: it was fortunate that Clementine and Sarah were there to divert and control him!

Picnics were the great distraction: Winston would work in the mornings, and then they would all set out for a picnic expedition into the foothills of the Atlas. This rather touching snapshot of Winston was taken during one of these expeditions. Gradually his vitality returned.

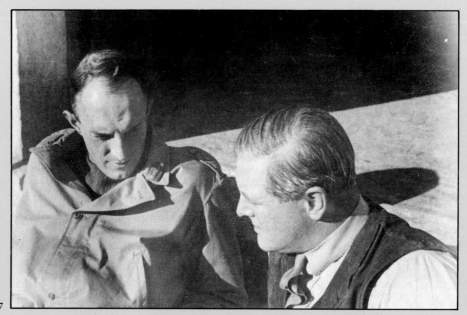

327

When Randolph had visited his father during his illness in North Africa, he had been awaiting orders
to be parachuted into Yugoslavia to join up with the British Military Mission attached to
Marshal Tito and his partisan forces. In February, Randolph was duly dropped in the desolate
mountain regions of Yugoslavia, and led a hazardous and spartan existence alongside the partisans.
Here he is with Brigadier Fitzroy Maclean, who headed the British Mission to Marshal Tito.

328

Winston, his family and entourage arrived back in England on 18 January 1944. He had been
away for just over two months; he had travelled many thousands of hazardous miles by
sea and air; he had celebrated his sixty-ninth birthday; he had survived a serious illness – it was
indeed good to have him safely home again. A few hours after his return, Winston went to the House
of Commons (now sitting in the House of Lords following the total destruction of the Chamber
by bombs in 1942). Here he received a heart-warming welcome – Members rose from their seats,
cheered and waved order papers.
Both Sarah and I went with our mother to witness our father's 'welcome home' from the
House of Commons.

329

Chequers continued to be a haven at weekends. There was a constant stream of colleagues, commanders and guests from overseas, but members of the family also foregathered whenever possible. Here is a family group at about this time.
Left to right (back row): Peregrine with his father Jack Churchill; (middle row): Pamela (Randolph's wife); Sarah; Duncan Sandys; (front row): Clementine; Winston; Diana.

330

Over and above all her concerns and duties as wife of the Prime Minister (and they were manifold), Clementine was ever faithful and energetic in working for her regular causes: the Aid to Russia Fund (which continued to boom); the Fulmer Chase Maternity Home; and, since 1941, the work of the Young Women's Christian Association (Y.W.C.A.) with which she was closely involved, becoming President of the Y.W.C.A. Wartime Fund. The special care of the 'Y.W.' during the war was to provide club and hostel facilities for the ever-increasing numbers of women war-workers, whether in the services, on the land, or in the factories. As was her wont, Clementine took her role as President of the Y.W.C.A. appeal very seriously, and not only helped the Association to raise a great deal of money, but also sought to raise the standards, despite wartime difficulties, in all the Y.W.C.A. clubs and hostels. Here is Clementine surrounded by a group of 'landgirls' – members of the Women's Land Army, after visiting their hostel.

Although the day and the hour were unknown except to a very few, everyone was aware that 1944 was the year in which the Allies must launch their assault across the Channel upon the fortress of Europe. This knowledge coloured thoughts and actions, and heightened perception. The British Isles teemed and bulged with troops and war materials. Everywhere large military exercises took place – training and practising for the fateful hour. People who had been wearied by the wear and tear of nearly five years of war were stimulated by the consciousness of the great and fearful events which must unfold: as the threat of invasion had called forth the best from all sorts and conditions of men and women, so now people bent their energies to whatever their tasks might be. They had borne so much – survived so much – they were not going to fail now.

331

During the weeks leading up to D-Day, Churchill spent much time visiting units of Allied military forces in training for this stupendous operation. Here, in this picture, Winston has momentarily turned away from the rank of young soldiers he is inspecting – his face is sombre.
It is not hard to guess the reason: Winston Churchill knew better than most people the grim ordeal these fine young men must face within the space of a few weeks – and for a moment he has turned away, overborne by his thoughts and feelings.

332

Churchill (wearing the uniform of a Colonel in the 4th Hussars) with General Eisenhower, who had been appointed Supreme Commander of the Allied Expeditionary Force in Western Europe.

TUESDAY, JUNE 6, 1944 · *Latest Prices* · BLACK OUT 10.57 to 5.0 · Moon Rises 9.50 p.m. Full Moon, Tonight · Sets 6.29 a.m. Radio Page 7 · LATE NIGHT

THE STAR

ALL GOING TO PLAN Says

333 · No. 17,459 · ONE PENNY

In the earliest hours of 6 June 1944 the Americans and British launched upon the Normandy coastline of France the greatest amphibious assault of all time. The attack involved 176,000 troops; 4,000 invasion craft; 11,000 aircraft; and 600 warships.

335

It can be imagined how Winston longed to be involved at close quarters with the great events in Europe, and at the first possible moment he paid a visit to Normandy with some eminent companions. Above left: Winston, with Field Marshal Smuts and Sir Alan Brooke on the bridge of a destroyer en route for the French coast. It was indeed a moving, thrilling moment for Winston when on 12 June he once more set foot upon the soil of France. Here he is greeted by 'Monty', now field commander of all land forces under Eisenhower.

336

Just over a month later Winston paid another visit to France. Here his car is surrounded by troops in the ruined city of Caen, which had proved a hard nut to crack.

337

Soon after D-Day, the Germans launched their secret weapon (V-1) — instantly dubbed 'Doodle-bugs' — against London. My battery was moved into the country as part of the redeployment of London's defences. One day, my parents 'dropped in' on us. During their visit there was an 'Alert'. Here a fellow-officer and myself are pointing out the 'doodle-bug' at which the guns are firing.

September 1944 saw the Second Quebec Conference, where Churchill and Roosevelt once more confabulated. Let us mark this Quebec Conference with a picture of a *female* 'Big Three'!
Left to right: Mrs Roosevelt; Princess Alice, Countess of Athlone (wife of the Governor General of Canada); Clementine Churchill.

339

General de Gaulle, now Head of the Provisional French Government, invited both Winston and Clementine to pay their first visit to liberated Paris for the ceremonies of Armistice Day, 11 November 1944. Winston's unshakeable friendship for, and championship of France and her people, made this visit particularly moving and significant.
After laying a wreath on the Tomb of the Unknown Warrior beneath the Arc de Triomphe, Churchill and the General walked together down the Champs-Elysées, cheered to the echo by crowds of Parisians.
Behind Churchill are (left to right): Duff Cooper (the British Ambassador); Anthony Eden; Georges Bidault (French Foreign Minister). Extreme right Sir Alan Brooke.

The last time Churchill and Roosevelt were destined to meet was at the Yalta 'Big Three' conference in the Crimea in early February 1945, for two months later the President was to die very suddenly. Churchill noticed a change in his great friend and colleague, and felt that his vitality was not as heretofore. But the news of his death on 12 April was a profound shock and grief to him.
Here is a picture of the 'Big Three' at what was their last meeting.
With hindsight one can see that Roosevelt looked frail.
Decisions taken at the Yalta conference have cast long and heavy shadows upon the lives of millions of people to this day. Britain's bargaining power was small in comparison to the weight of the 'big battalions', and Roosevelt and his advisers were out of tune with much of British thinking on many of the most vital matters concerning, particularly, the Eastern European peoples: and the President sought to conciliate Stalin on many issues.
Churchill came away deeply disturbed by much that had been decided.

340

341

The Conference is over for the day: empty teacups, overflowing ashtrays are the remains of a long and, no doubt arduous, session. But Churchill and Roosevelt stay on together . . . they had so many important things to discuss and, unknown to them, time was indeed short. It had been a remarkable friendship, 'forged in the fire of war', as Winston was to put it in his message to Mrs Roosevelt later. Their close liaison had started with the famous exchange of secret letters between the President and 'Naval Person' and later 'Former Naval Person' (F.D.R.'s way of addressing the letters, in reference to Winston's tenure as First Lord of the Admiralty). They had actually met on ten different occasions between 1941, and this last meeting at Yalta. Seldom can a friendship and a meeting of minds have portended so much for the lives of millions of people.

On 23 March 1945, the British and American armies began their crossing of the Rhine – the last great natural barrier between these advancing armies and Germany's heartland. Churchill (naturally) wanted to witness this dramatic leap forward, and spent several days with 'Ike' and 'Monty' at their advanced headquarters. On 25 March he himself crossed the Rhine with Monty. On their return, they visited the ruined railway bridge at Wesel, where Winston is seen (above) scrambling over the debris: their visit was curtailed when the bridge came under heavy shell-fire. The next day Winston picnicked on the banks of the Rhine with 'Brookie' (Field Marshal Sir Alan Brooke) and Monty. (Note the coats flung on the ground, a hamper for a table, and Winston's stick planted firmly in the ground). But it was not all snacks with Field Marshals: below right, Winston enjoys a nice cup of tea with British troops.

By April 1945, 'Mrs Churchill's Aid to Russia Fund' had collected £6,700,000, and in the spring of that year she was invited by the Russian Red Cross to go to Russia on a goodwill visit. With her on this thrilling six-week journey went her own private secretary, Miss Grace Hamblin, and Miss Mabel Johnson, the Secretary to the Aid to Russia Fund. Excited though she was by the prospect of this journey, Clementine felt deeply reluctant to leave Winston at this time, when every hour seemed to bring news of dramatic events. Clementine arrived in Moscow on 2 April – the day after her sixtieth birthday. While in Moscow, she was received not only by Mr Molotov (Soviet Commissar for Foreign Affairs), but also by Marshal Stalin himself. Clementine then set out on a long and unforgettable journey through Russia, travelling in a special train. She and her party visited Leningrad, Stalingrad; towns in the Caucasus; and Rostov-on-Don (where her Fund was completely re-equipping two hospitals). She visited Yalta and Sebastopol in the Crimea, Odessa and Kursk. Everywhere she went, Clementine received a warm and enthusiastic reception.

When Clementine arrived back in Moscow on 5 May, she had to catch up with many crucial events. Various 'news flashes' had been relayed spasmodically to her during her journey – but she had felt very out of touch. During this period, events had succeeded one another with stunning rapidity: President Roosevelt had died; the Russians had reached Berlin; Mussolini had been executed by the partisans; the German forces in Italy had surrendered; and on 30 April, Hitler had shot himself in the bunker in the Chancellery. Clementine was in Moscow when the news was received of the unconditional surrender of the German forces on all fronts. Her heart ached at being apart from Winston at this triumphant hour. On Victory-in-Europe Day, she sent him a cable: 'All my thoughts are with you on this supreme day my darling. It could not have happened without you.' Before leaving Moscow, the Soviet Government decorated her with the Order of the Red Banner of Labour. Clementine arrived home on 12 May, and was met at the airfield by an overjoyed Winston. In the pictures below, Clementine is seen during her journeyings with (left) the Chairman of the Anti-Fascist Committee of Soviet Women and (right) Miss Johnson, in a young people's camp in the Crimea.

The Daily Telegraph
and Morning Post

No. 28,048 LONDON, WEDNESDAY, MAY 9, 1945 Printed in LONDON and MANCHESTER PRICE 1½d.

NATION'S VE OUTBURST OF JOY: ALL-NIGHT CELEBRATIONS

ROYAL FAMILY FIVE TIMES OUT ON PALACE BALCONY

Mr. CHURCHILL: 'NO GREATER

VAST CROWDS HAIL THE KING AT PALACE

MR. CHURCHILL'S V SIGN FROM BALCONY

British family instinct inspired tens of thousands of men and

FROM EARLY MORNING vast crowds, celebrating VE-Day, waited outside Buckingham Palace in hopes of seeing their King and Queen.

Their wish was gratified in the afternoon when their Majesties, accompanied by Princess Elizabeth and Princess Margaret, appeared on the balcony and acknowledged with smiles their tumultuous reception.

On the second of their subsequent appearances on the balcony, they came out with Mr. Churchill who was greeted with wild expressions of delight, informality and good-fellowship with the rejoicing people were the message of the King's wave of the hand and the happy smiles of the Queen and the Premier.

GERMANS FIGHT

GERMAN FLEET TO GO TO ALLIED PORTS

ADMIRALTY ORDER

The Admiralty announced yesterday that the following orders have been issued for the surrender of the German Fleet: All German and German-controlled warships, auxiliary merchant ships and other at sea are being report their posit

2.40 a.m. SURRENDER SCENE AT ALLIED H.Q.

DRAMATIC 15 MINUTES THAT ENDED WAR

HUMBLED GERMANS

From DOUGLAS WILLIAMS, Daily Telegraph Special Correspondent

RHEIMS, Tuesday.

Europe is ov

On the balcony at Buckingham Palace on Victory-in-Europe Day, 8 May 1945. The King and Queen invited Winston Churchill to join them on the balcony with Princess Elizabeth (now eighteen and an officer in the A.T.S.) and Princess Margaret as they were cheered by an enormous crowd below.

Winston, surrounded by cheering crowds, making his way with difficulty down Whitehall to the House of Commons on VE-Day.

Daily Mirror

MAY 8

Tuesday, May 8, 1945
No. 12,911   ONE PENNY
Registered at G.P.O. as a Newspaper.

VE-DAY !

IT'S OVER IN THE WEST

TODAY is VE-Day—the day for which the British people have fought and endured five years, eight months and four days of war.

With unconditional surrender accepted by Germany's last remaining leaders, the war in Europe is over except for the actions of fanatical Nazis in isolated pockets, such as Prague.

The Prime Minister will make an official announcement—in accordance with arrangements between Britain, Russia and the U.S.—at 3 o'clock this afternoon. ALL TODAY AND TO-MORROW ARE PUBLIC HOLIDAYS IN BRITAIN, IN CELEBRATION OF OUR VICTORY.

We also remember and salute with gratitude and pride the men and women who suffered and died to make triumph possible — and the men still battling in the East against another cruel enemy who is still in the field.

War winners broadcast today

You will hear the voices of the King, Field-Marshals Montgomery and Alexander, and General Eisenhower when they broadcast over the B.B.C. Home Service tonight.

After the King's speech, at 9 p.m., and separated from it by the news bulletin, comes "Victory Report," a special programme which will contain the recorded voices of Ike and Monty, and other famous personalities of the war.

Additional features of the B.B.C. Home programme, which will end at 2 a.m. to-morrow, include, at 8 p.m., an address by the Archbishop of Canterbury at a Thanksgiving Service for Victory, and at 8.30 a tribute to the King.

★ VE-SCENE ★

TRAFALGAR SQUARE

It was a high old time in Trafalgar-square last night. Everybody wanted to climb something. This party of Wrens and Allied soldiers celebrated by clambering on to the lions. Army policemen present—like Nelson on his column—turned a blind eye.

London had joy night

"Daily Mirror" Reporter

PICCADILLY CIRCUS, VE-EVE. THIS is IT—and we are all going nuts! There are thousands of us in Piccadilly-circus. The police say more than 10,000—and that's a conservative estimate.

We are dancing the Conga and the jig and "Knees up, Mother Brown," and we are singing and whistling, and blowing paper trumpets.

The idea is to make a noise. We are. Even above the roar of the motors of low-flying bombers "shooting up" the city.

We are dancing around Eros in the black-out, but there is a glow from a bonfire up Shaftesbury-avenue and a news reel cinema has lit its canopy lights for the first time in getting on for six years.

A huge V sign glares down over Leicester Square. And gangs of girls and soldiers of all the Allied nations are waving rattles and shouting and climbing lamp-posts and swarming over cars that have become bogged down in this struggling, swirling mass of celebrating Londoners.

We have been waiting from two o'clock to celebrate. We went home at six when it seemed that the news of VE-Day would never come, but we are back now.

And on a glorious night we are making the most of it. A paper-hatted throng is trying to pull me out of this telephone box now. I hold the door tight, but the din from Piccadilly Circus is drowning my voice.

It is past midnight. We are still singing. A group of men liberated from German prison camps are yelling—"Roll out the Barrel."

"We sang it when we went to France in 1939 and we sang it as we tried to get out in 1940," they told me. "Now we sing it for victory."

Amid terrific cheers a New Zealand sailor climbed on the bonnet of a bus and from there to the roof.

He stood there swaying above the crowds as the American army swarmed up

◆ *Continued on Back Page*

Post-war fortunes

351

Churchill had always hoped that the Coalition Government would continue in existence until the defeat of all our enemies: but soon after VE-Day, it became clear that the wartime unity between the political parties would not hold until the defeat of Japan. The Labour Party having indicated that it would not continue in the Coalition, Churchill resigned as Prime Minister on 23 May: the King at once asked him to form an interim administration – the Caretaker Government – to bridge the period until the Dissolution of Parliament and the ensuing General Election had taken place. There was widespread speculation as to the election result: opinion polls were a relatively new feature in this country but the Gallup Poll (not widely published) had already shown for some time that Labour led the Conservatives. Opinion polls, however, were very incomplete inasmuch as they could not canvas the views of the three million service men and women, and there was a general assumption both in Britain and abroad that the Conservative Party, with Winston Churchill as its Leader, would win the day. Winston, although a politically combatant animal, found it hard to exchange the role of leader of a united government and nation, for that of, once more, a party political figure; and particularly in his early election speeches, he did not have the right feel for the mood of the electorate. As for Clementine, she wished Winston would now retire, and not re-enter the lists of divisive party politics. But Winston was very far away from any thought of retirement.

352

During the election campaign Churchill made extensive speaking tours throughout the country:
everywhere large cheering crowds greeted him – but now one knows that many thousands
who turned out to salute their wartime leader, voted against his party in the polling booths.
A unique feature of this election was that, in order that the forces still serving scattered
throughout the world might vote, a three-week gap was imposed between polling day (5 July)
and the count and declaration of the poll (26 July), thus enabling the service votes
to be gathered in from overseas.
Here, in this picture, Winston is addressing a street meeting during a tour in his own constituency.
during a tour in his own constituency.

353

During part of the three-week period between polling day and the declaration of the poll, Winston and Clementine went to France for a holiday, taking me with them. We were the guests of General Brutinel (of French-Scottish descent) at the Chateau de Bordaberry near Hendaye, on the Spanish frontier. These days of 'limbo' passed pleasantly enough – my father taking up his paint-brushes once more, and my mother and I happy with sightseeing. Here my parents are glimpsed on the beach at Hendaye. But over us hung the tantalising cloud of uncertainty: what secret did the ballot boxes hold?

The Potsdam Conference – the first meeting of the Big Three to take place since victory in Europe – was planned for 17 July to 2 August, and would thus straddle the declaration of the results of the General Election. But no time could be lost: it was vital for the leaders of the Allies to confer upon the immense and pressing problems now looming in the wake of victory. Since during the time of the Conference there might be a change in the British Premiership, Churchill insisted that Mr Clement Attlee (the Leader of the Labour Party and Deputy Prime Minister) should attend the meetings too – so that in any event there would be no dislocation or precious time lost in re-briefing. The Conference was held in a pleasant and unscarred suburb of Potsdam: the houses allocated to the President and the British Prime Minister were soon renamed 'The White House' and 'No. 10 Downing Street'. Churchill was anxious to 'get on terms' as soon as possible with Roosevelt's successor, President Harry Truman (who up to now had been very much the background figure Vice-Presidents usually are). From their first meeting Winston liked and respected Truman.

Daily Mail
NO. 15,358   ONE PENNY   **FOR KING AND EMPIRE**   FRIDAY, JULY 27, 1945

LABOUR Government, 416: OPPOSITION, 211—MAJORITY, 205

CHURCHILL RESIGNS: ATTLEE FORMING HIS CABINET

New Premier may go back to 'Big 3' alone

By WILSON BROADBENT, *Political Correspondent*

MR. WINSTON CHURCHILL drove to Buckingham Palace early yesterday evening very soon after Labour's mounting victories at the polls had reached their sensational climax. Formally tendering his resignation as Prime Minister, he

Still smiling

PM HINTS AT QUICK PEACE
Churchill gives thanks to peo...

3 Powers send an ultimatum to the Japs
SURRENDER—OR RUIN

RESULT STUNS WORLD
'Friendship will go on'—Moscow

THIS election result will probably have more immediate repercussions over a wider area of the world than any other of the century.

Of Britain's two great Allies, Russia received it calmly, with the conviction that existing friendship would be maintained; the

On 26 July the votes were counted: Winston and his colleagues had returned from Potsdam two days before to be on the spot. By noon on the 26th it was clear that the Socialists had won a landslide victory over all other parties. Whatever their political opinions, most people in Britain were amazed by the result of the Election, but abroad, where literally millions saw in Winston Churchill the symbol of their deliverance and the champion of freedom, people were aghast at what appeared to be a monstrous act of ingratitude. Winston himself was stunned and deeply wounded; but both he and Clementine hid their feelings behind a stoic mien. These lines from Rudyard Kipling's famous poem 'If' seemed particularly appropriate at this time:

'If you can meet with Triumph and Disaster
And treat those two impostors just the same . . .'

Clementine did not dally – here (below) removals men are at work outside No. 10 on 1 August. In the autumn of 1945, Winston and Clementine bought a house in a cul-de-sac in Kensington: No. 28 Hyde Park Gate. It does not look very special outside, but it was charming inside, and it had a delightful garden. Here, then, Winston and Clementine were to live for the next twenty years: and here, peacefully, one cold winter's morning, he was to die.
Bottom right: Clementine's bedroom and balcony.

355

And there was always Chartwell – in good times or in bad, Chartwell never failed him, and it was the place he most liked to be in all the world. Clementine set to work at once to open up the house again, making sensible labour-saving alterations. Soon after the Election, Winston went for a holiday to Italy, taking Sarah with him; Clementine stayed at home to grapple with Chartwell.

They stayed in a villa on Lake Como, lent by his kind and gallant friend Field Marshal 'Alex'. Winston painted, and made expeditions – and inevitably brooded. Both he and Clementine had taken the result of the Election 'hard': how could they not? But the world saw only the proud and smiling exterior. And it *was* ironic – because everywhere he went at home people smiled and cheered and waved; theatre audiences rose to their feet clapping; letters poured in! It was touching – and it was balm: but the bruise remained a long time. My mother put it so well in a letter to me: 'The crowds shout "Churchill for ever" and "We want Churchill". But all the King's horses and all the King's men can't put Humpty Dumpty together again.' But Winston was not one to dwell on defeat: very soon he was back, taking his place in the House of Commons as Leader of the Opposition; and in the country as Leader of the Conservatives he made great speeches rallying the Tories to recovery, and action – and eventually to victory once more. On the home front he started farming, and as well as his paint-brushes, took up his pen again to indite his record of these last stern and glorious years.

Soon the formerly occupied countries of Europe (and others throughout the world) began inviting Winston to pay them official visits; and during the next few years he was to go to many countries to receive the highest honours, and be laden with gifts. Those of us who accompanied him on these occasions will never forget the tumultuous scenes of joy which greeted Winston wherever he went, from vast crowds who had often waited long hours just to glimpse and hail their hero.

In November 1945, Churchill went to Belgium at the invitation of the Prince Regent and the Government. Teeming crowds thronged the streets of Brussels and Antwerp, and lined the roadside between the cities. Here in Brussels, Winston stands up in his car to receive the cheers of the people. Banners and groups of *anciens combattants* throng the corner.

359

In May 1946, Winston and Clementine visited the Netherlands, and were received with much honour by Queen Wilhelmina, her Government and people. The Dutch had suffered greatly in the war, particularly as a result of near starvation during the last winter: now they cheered and cheered.

Here (left) my parents and myself are with Princess (later Queen) Juliana and Prince Bernhard and their children at the palace of Soestdyjk. The little Princesses (left to right) are: Princess Beatrix, aged eight (she is now Queen); Princess Margriet, aged three, and Princess Irene, aged six.

360

361

In March 1946, Churchill made a speech at Westminster College, Fulton, Missouri, which
attracted world-wide attention (and sharp criticism in some quarters). In his address, Churchill
pointed to the insidious and ever-increasing Soviet domination of Eastern Europe:
he used the vivid phrase 'the iron curtain', which now is a commonplace of modern vocabulary.
While in the USA, Winston and Clementine made a visit to Mrs Roosevelt at Hyde Park.
Winston laid a wreath on the grave of his friend and valiant comrade-in-war.
Here, with Clementine and Mrs Roosevelt, he stands in sombre contemplation.

362

Switzerland, although neutral throughout the war, soon hastened to show where the hearts of most of
her people lay. A group of Swiss friends and admirers placed at Winston's disposal a charming house
on the shores of Lac Leman at Choisy (about half way between Geneva and Lausanne). Here Winston,
Clementine and members of their family passed some carefree weeks. Later, Winston was received
officially in Geneva, Berne, Lausanne and Zurich, the Swiss abandoning all their reserve to applaud
him wherever he went. At Zurich University on 19 September 1946, Churchill made a speech which
has come to be regarded as the foundation stone in the long and laborious task of building a united
Europe. Urging reconciliation, he said: 'We must all turn our backs upon the horrors of the past. We
must look to the future. We cannot afford to drag forward across the years that are to come the
hatreds and revenges which have sprung from the injuries of the past. If Europe is to be saved from
infinite misery, and indeed from final doom, there must be an act of faith in the European family and
an act of oblivion against all the crimes and follies of the past.'

363

Clementine now, most deservedly, came into her own share of public recognition: in 1946 she was made Dame Grand Cross of the Order of the British Empire, on the recommendation of the Labour Prime Minister, Clement Attlee. During this summer also she received honorary degrees from Glasgow and Oxford Universities. Winston was so proud and pleased that his 'Clemmie''s contribution should win her praise and honours: 'A little bit of sugar for the bird!' he would say delightedly. This portrait was painted by the American artist Chandor in 1946.
It shows that at the age of sixty-one, Clementine was still elegant and beautiful.

364

On 8 June 1946 there was a great Victory Parade. Although no longer Prime Minister, Winston was treated with due honour, and placed alongside the Dominion Prime Ministers at the foot of the royal dais in the Mall from which the King took the salute.
Waiting for the pageant to start, Winston chats to Mr Mackenzie King, Prime Minister of Canada; (left) Mr Attlee studies the programme; (right) Field Marshal Smuts, Prime Minister of South Africa.

In 1941 the King had appointed Winston Churchill to be Lord Warden of the Cinque Ports, the 158th holder of that ancient office: but it was only in August 1946 that his installation took place at Dover. The office of Lord Warden has existed for nearly a thousand years; the original Cinque Ports were Hastings, Romney, Hythe, Dover and Sandwich, and their duty was to provide ships to defend the realm. Now an honourable sinecure with a magnificent and very elaborate uniform, it involves a ceremonial which is centuries old – yet it all seemed to have a special meaning when set against the starkness of the dangers this country had faced so recently. Certainly Winston Churchill seemed a fit person for this honourable and ancient office. 'We install as Lord Warden,' said the Archbishop of Canterbury in his address in Dover's beautiful little church of St Mary-in-the-Castle, 'one who, in the years of our greatest peril and need, kept watch and ward over England, over the Empire, and over freedom.'

Winston greatly relished this appointment, which he held until his death; the Lord Warden's flag flew over Chartwell, and his car always bore the Lord Warden's pennant. The picture shows Winston acknowledging the cheers of the crowds as he is driven from Dover Castle to the marquee in the town where his installation took place.

366

In February 1947 I married Christopher Soames – he was twenty-six and I was twenty-four.
Christopher was a captain in the Coldstream Guards; having 'done the war' from Cairo through the
Western Desert to Tunis, he had then opted for service with an Intelligence unit and had operated in
Italy and France. The war over, he was appointed Assistant Military Attaché in Paris, which was
where I met him in September 1946. My father took to him instantly, and their friendship grew into a
most warm and moving relationship. My mother was a slower conquest, but she too became devoted
to 'The Chimp', as he was known in our family. We were married on a grey, bitterly cold day in
St Margaret's, Westminster, where my parents, too, had started their long and happy marriage.
My only bridesmaid was my cousin and greatest friend, Judy Montagu.

367

Twelve days after all the family joy and excitement over my marriage, Winston's brother Jack
Churchill died: he was sixty-seven. Throughout their lives Winston and Jack had been devoted to one
another, and even during the swift tempo of life in the war they had seen each other very often. Jack's
death deeply grieved both Winston and Clementine, and saddened us all. Although he was by nature
retiring, Uncle Jack's departure made a void in our family circle. In this photograph, taken during the
war, the two brothers are attending a mock battle.

368

In 1946, Winston bought the farm which adjoined his property down the hill from Chartwell, and for the next eleven years he derived much pleasure and interest from farming. Christopher and I had come to live in the Chartwell Farm house and, since Christopher had left the army soon after our marriage, Winston asked him to be his farm manager. We both rode and hunted quite often, and fired by our example (although he had really given up riding years ago) Winston was determined to have another go! So when the Old Surrey and Burstow hounds met at Chartwell Farm shortly before his seventy-fourth birthday in 1948, Winston hired a horse from Mr Sam Marsh's livery stables, and came out with us all for an hour or two. It really was quite an achievement: but we were all deeply relieved when, having made his point, Winston did not make a habit of riding again.

After the war Chartwell life soon picked up again and, especially in the summer, people came for the day. Here (below right) a wise and trusted friend and counsellor, Lord Camrose (proprietor of the *Daily Telegraph* and *Sunday Telegraph*) is with Winston, Sarah and Randolph beside the goldfish pool. And (below left) another regular visitor on his trips to Europe – Bernard M. Baruch – the eminent American financier and elder statesman, strolls on the lawn with Winston in summer 1949. Their friendship dated from the First World War when Baruch was on the American War Industries Board, and Churchill was Minister of Munitions.

369

370

After his defeat in 1945, Winston lost no time in starting to write his war memoirs:
the six volumes appeared between 1948 and 1954. 'The Moral of the Work'
(which was printed at the beginning of each volume) was:

In War: Resolution
In Defeat: Defiance
In Victory: Magnanimity
In Peace: Goodwill.

It could really stand as the theme of his whole life.
Apart from all these activities, he was, of course, fully engaged in political life as Leader
of the Opposition, and Leader of the Conservative Party which, during these years, saw a
veritable renaissance of thought, policy and vigour under the guidance of such men as
Lord Woolton and Rab (later Lord) Butler. Nor were Winston's political interests and
activities confined to these shores: pursuing the European theme he had expounded first
at Zurich in 1946, he kept closely in touch with the European Movement.

371

In August 1949 Winston went to Strasbourg to attend the Inaugural Session of the
Consultative Assembly of the Council of Europe. On the night of 12 August Churchill
addressed a crowd of 15,000 people in the main square at Strasbourg: he spoke in
French, and was cheered to the echo. Here he is seen in earnest conversation with
Monsieur Paul Henri Spaak, Belgian's Foreign Minister, who was the President of the
Consultative Assembly. Part of the great crowd in the square beneath can be seen
through the open window.

Randolph and Pamela Digby's marriage had ended in divorce in 1945, when their only child, Winston, was five years old. In November 1948 Randolph married again, to June Osborne. A year later she bore a beautiful child – Arabella. Here is a family group at Arabella's christening in December 1949. Left to right: Randolph; Clementine; Winston; June with Arabella; and June's parents, Colonel and Mrs Rex Osborne.

Sarah and Vic Oliver had been divorced in 1945, and later that year she was demobilised from the W.A.A.F. and returned to a busy career on the stage and screen. Soon after the war Sarah met a gifted photographer, Antony Beauchamp, and they came to love each other. Sarah went out to the United States in the summer of 1949 to play the leading role in *The Philadelphia Story*: presently Antony followed her and they were married on 18 October at Sea Island, Georgia, when Sarah had a few days off from her play. Sad to relate, neither of Sarah's parents came to like Antony – although Clementine made a great effort to do so. But whatever their feelings about the marriage, Sarah's relationship with her parents remained strong and warm. Both Winston and Clementine truly grieved for Sarah when difficulties arose between her and Antony. After some temporary separations Sarah and Antony finally parted for good in 1955.

374

Winston now embarked on a new venture: he bought a racehorse! My husband Christopher (who had always loved riding, hunting and racing, and had a modest horse himself) introduced Winston to the fun and tantalizing anxieties of flat racing. Taking good advice, Christopher was instrumental in Winston buying (in the summer of 1949) a grey three-year-old colt – Colonist II. Winston registered Lord Randolph Churchill's colours (pink, chocolate sleeves and cap), and the horse was sent to Walter Nightingall's racing stables at Epsom. Before he was sold to stud three years later, Colonist had carried his owner's colours to victory thirteen times, and won for him handsome sums in prize-money.

Winston came to own several more racehorses, and eventually bought a small stud farm at Newchapel Green, near Lingfield. Here he bred two well-known winners – Vienna and High Hat. Winston was made a member of the Jockey Club in 1950 – a distinction he greatly relished.

375

Winston and Clementine now had quite a tally of grandchildren – seven to date. Here is a picture taken at Chartwell in September 1951. Clementine has annotated it herself. Duncan and Diana's two daughters are not here, but Julian Sandys (born 1936) and Nicholas Soames (born 1948) are sitting on the ground. Winston has Emma Soames (born 1949) on his lap. Then comes 'young' Winston Churchill (born 1940), and Clementine, talking to Arabella Churchill (born 1949).

376

377

Evening Standard

FRIDAY, OCTOBER 26, 1951 · Three-halfpence

39,647

No great Right swing, but Tories gain nine more seats

WINSTON IN POWER

Working majority but a small one

LIBERAL DEBACLE

State of Parties	
CONSERVATIVES	290
NATIO	14

In February 1950 there was a General Election, and the great Socialist majority slumped to 5. The Labour Government staggered on with this slender majority for another nineteen months, and then went to the country again in October 1951. This time the Conservatives were returned with an overall majority of 17 seats: it was a moment of justifiable triumph for them after the crushing defeat six years before. This victory marked the start of thirteen years of Tory rule. Winston waged a most energetic campaign. Clementine valiantly held the fort for him at Woodford; while he toured the country speaking at meetings and rallies. The photograph above shows them both at a Committee Rooms' window. Winston's health and strength were really amazing; since 1945 he had had few illnesses, although in 1949 he had sustained a minor stroke which had escaped public attention. He was now rather deaf – but fill of vim and vigour. His party were proud of him and rallied behind his leadership. On 26 October the King sent for Winston Churchill and asked him to form a government. At seventy-six he was Prime Minister again, and the picture opposite shows him jubilant, on his day of victory.

Shortly before the General Election in October 1951 King George VI had undergone a major operation for the removal of a lung. Although recovered enough to attend to affairs of state at home, the visit to Australia and New Zealand which he and the Queen had planned to make that autumn was cancelled. In the New Year, Princess Elizabeth and the Duke of Edinburgh set out on a Commonwealth tour. They were in Kenya when they were told of the King's death in his sleep in the early hours of 6 February; he was fifty-six. Princess Elizabeth, now in her twenty-sixth year, became Queen. She at once returned to England, and this memorable and moving picture shows her descending the aircraft steps to be greeted by her Prime Minister, Winston Churchill, and members of his Cabinet. Winston was deeply affected by the death of the King – bonds of friendship as well as fidelity and respect had been forged between Sovereign and Prime Minister during the hard years of war. But now the accession of the young Queen Elizabeth II aroused all Churchill's sense of chivalry and history. He had served five sovereigns as soldier, minister and counsellor, and now he was to become the young Queen's devoted servant. With tears in his eyes, he would remind us that Britain had always been fortunate under her Queens.

In August 1952 an event took place which caused much pleasure and rejoicing in our family circle: Winston's niece, Jack and Goonie's only daughter Clarissa, married Anthony Eden, for long a friend and colleague of Winston's, and now Foreign Secretary in his Government. (Anthony Eden's first marriage had been dissolved in 1950.) Winston and Clementine gave a wedding breakfast for Anthony and Clarissa at No. 10. Here is the wedding group: Standing (left to right): John Eden (Bridegroom's nephew); Sir Timothy Eden (brother); the Bridegroom; Antony Beauchamp; W.S.C.; Peregrine Spencer Churchill; John Spencer Churchill (Clarissa's brother); Duncan Sandys; Diana; Mrs Peter Negretti (Bridegroom's niece). On sofa: Clementine; the Bride; myself; Sarah.

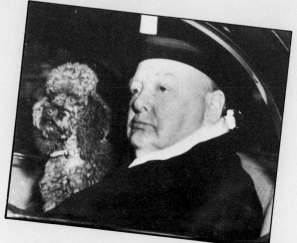

Winston was greatly attached to a chocolate-coloured poodle – Rufus. Sadly, Rufus was run over by a bus on Brighton sea-front (he was attending the Conservative Party Conference with his master when he met this untimely end). So a kind friend gave Winston Rufus-the-Second, who stars in this picture. He appears to be greatly enjoying the limelight.

382

In October 1952, Winston made his 'Prime Minister's visit' to the Queen at Balmoral. Here he is with the Queen, Prince Charles and Princess Anne.

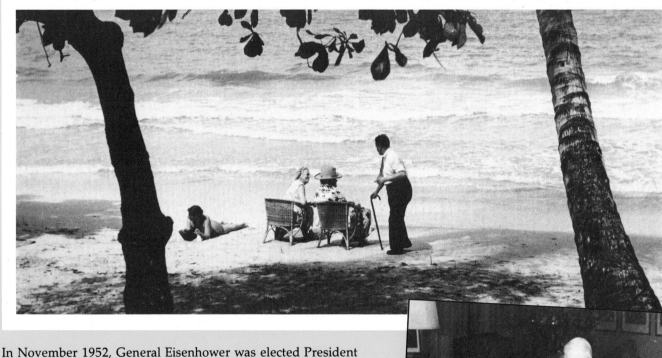

383

In November 1952, General Eisenhower was elected President of the United States. In the New Year of 1953, Winston went to America with the prime purpose of consulting with the President-elect and also to call upon the outgoing President, Mr Truman. While in New York, Winston and Clementine stayed with his great old friend, Bernard Baruch. The two men are seen (right) in conversation with General Eisenhower. After their American visit, Winston and Clementine went for a sunshine holiday to Jamaica, taking Christopher and me with them; we all stayed near Ocho Rios. Winston made an official visit to Kingston, and received a tumultuous welcome. Otherwise, painting and beach life was the order of the day. In the picture above Winston and Clementine are playing 'King and Queen Canute' on the beach at Prospect. The recumbent figure is myself.

384

1953 was Coronation Year – and great were the preparations and celebrations! In April the Queen honoured her Prime Minister, Winston Churchill, by conferring upon him the Order of the Garter, one of the oldest orders of chivalry, and in the personal gift of the Sovereign. Winston and Clementine went to Windsor Castle where the Queen invested him with the Order. Winston was truly moved and gratified by this special mark of distinction and favour from his Sovereign.

Coronation Day was 2 June – it was wet and drizzling, but nothing could dampen the spirits or cheers of the hundreds of thousands of people who lined the route of the procession, many of whom had slept out on the pavements the previous night. This was the third Coronation that Winston and Clementine had attended together; they drove in a coach in the procession, with a mounted escort of the 4th Hussars (Winston's old regiment). This picture shows them leaving No. 10 for the ceremony. Winston is wearing the uniform of Lord Warden of the Cinque Ports, and round his neck are the chain and badge of the Order of the Garter. Accompanying him to the door are Nicholas and Emma Soames. My parents had invited all the grandchildren to spend the day at No. 10, and to watch the procession from windows in Whitehall; they also had the fun of seeing their grandparents so wonderfully dressed up for the occasion. This lovely photograph of my mother in 'full sail' shows her in the mantle of a Dame Grand Cross of the Order of the British Empire: the mantle is strikingly beautiful, being of vivid petunia satin, lined with pearl grey.

387

Three weeks after the Coronation, Winston suffered a stroke. It happened towards the end of an official dinner at No. 10 given in honour of the Italian Prime Minister. It was barely perceptible, and only a few of us realised that something was amiss. On being told that his host was greatly fatigued, Signor de Gasperi was most understanding, and departed early. The effects of the stroke were more pronounced the next day, although, amazingly, Winston presided at a Cabinet meeting without his colleagues realising he had been stricken. Then he retreated to Chartwell, and thereafter the symptoms worsened considerably. A public statement soon had to be made, particularly as a conference in Bermuda between President Eisenhowever, Churchill and the French Premier was impending. The statement made no mention of a stroke – merely stating that the Prime Minister was in need of 'a complete rest'. The weeks that followed were anxious indeed: but immured at Chartwell, Winston was safe from prying eyes, and those who knew the true situation kept their counsel. Gradually his condition improved, and strength and mobility returned. Very soon he started seeing papers again, and keeping in general touch with affairs. Almost two months after his stroke, Winston presided at a Cabinet meeting again. But the real challenge on the horizon, and the goal to which he determinedly set himself, was the Conservative Party Conference in early October, when as Leader he would have to make a major speech. Winston knew well that the audience would include eagle-eyed journalists from the world's press. For him so much hung on this occasion: we held our breath – he triumphed.

388

Winston addressing the Conference: to his right are Anthony Eden and Clementine.

390

To add to his other honours, it was announced in October 1953 that Winston had been awarded the Nobel Prize for Literature. Winston was immensely gratified that his 'other' profession had been recognized in this way. The Nobel Prizegiving ceremony is always held in December in Stockholm, and the date (10 December) clashed with the re-convened Bermuda Conference which had been postponed from the summer because of Winston's illness. It was obvious, therefore, that he could not go himself to collect this glittering and prestigious prize. However, Clementine was invited to receive the award on his behalf. Here she is, with King Gustav of. Sweden, who has made the presentation. Far away across the world, Churchill was conferring with President Eisenhower and the French Premier.

Lady Dorothea Head (later Viscountess Head), who with her husband Anthony (a distinguished soldier and ministerial colleague) were close friends of Winston and Clementine, is a gifted artist: she painted this enchanting study of Winston. Clementine's letter shows what she thought of it.

391

April 15 · 1952
10. Downing Street.
London, S.W.1.

My dear Dot,
I'm so much pleased that you have sent me a photograph of the really delightful painting of Winston It's full of character & shows him at his most loveable. I'm having it framed for the Shelf where I keep my special favourites in a row.

Yours affectionate
Clementine S.C.

392

Winston had been invested by the Queen as a Knight of the Garter in the previous year, and now in the summer of 1954 he was installed at the beautiful and ancient service held yearly and attended by the Sovereign and the Knights in St George's Chapel within the walls of Windsor Castle. Here each living Knight of the Garter has his stall, above which is hung his Garter Banner. After a Knight's death, his Banner is 'laid up' in a moving ceremonial, and given back to the Knight's family.
Winston Churchill's banner now hangs in his study at Chartwell.
Here is Winston in the glorious robes of a Knight of the Garter on 14 June 1954, the day of his installation. The Knights, with those about to be installed, process down the hill from Windsor Castle to the Chapel, with the Sovereign and other members of the Royal Family: it is a most splendid sight.

393

This picture of Nellie Romilly, Clementine's sister, was taken at Chartwell in 1954: the following February she died of cancer. Nellie's life had never been easy: her war-wounded husband had been delicate, and they were badly off financially; their sons, Giles and Esmond (upon whom she doted), were a constant source of worry: during the war Giles was a prisoner-of-war, and Esmond (a pilot) was killed on a bombing raid. But despite many difficulties Nellie was always gay and buoyant. Although the two sisters were very different in character and temperament, there was between them a strong bond of affection and loyalty, and Winston was always devoted to 'Nellinita' as he called her.

On 30 November 1954 Winston was eighty, and as his birthday approached he was showered with presents and messages. Thousands of people both in Britain and overseas contributed to an Eightieth Birthday Presentation Fund, of which the grand total was £295,000! Winston made this wonderful sum into a trust fund, the largest contribution from which went towards the founding of Churchill College, Cambridge. The Queen and Prince Phillip, and members of the Royal Family, gave him four beautiful wine coasters.

Both Houses of Parliament formed an All-Party Committee, and joined in presenting Winston with his portrait executed by Graham Sutherland.

On 30 November members of both Houses of Parliament and their guests assembled in Westminster Hall, where the presentation was made. There can, perhaps, never have been such an occasion, where both Houses and all parties joined to do such singular honour to one of their own. Winston was most deeply moved. After the speeches, he and Clementine walked through the applauding throng in historic Westminster Hall to be greeted outside by cheering crowds.

That evening we, his family and close friends celebrated the great day at No. 10. The giant cake – a beautiful and intricate confection with pink and white icing – was a present from the firm of Floris. Surrounded by eighty candles, it bore a banner scroll on which were written the Shakespearian lines:

> Take him all in all he is a man. We shall
> Not look upon his like again . . .

And maybe we never shall.

There is an unfortunate postscript to this episode: Winston took a violent dislike to the portrait – he thought it odious and insulting. Clementine came to share his feelings about it; consequently it was never hung in their home. The picture so preyed on Winston's mind, that, unknown to him, Clementine had it destroyed. But the thought behind the gesture and presentation always gave Winston great and lasting gratification.

MANCHESTER GUARDIAN

No. 33,833 WEDNESDAY APRIL 6 1955 Price 3d

SIR WINSTON CHURCHILL RESIGNS

Sir Anthony Eden to See the Queen To-day

THE FINAL CABINET

Sir Winston Ch... ...ill has resigned. Yesterday he ...the last time... ...Prime...

To the Palace and Back

SIR WINSTON'S COMPOSURE

From our London Staff

Sir Winston arrived at Buckingham Palace at 4.32, looking more at ease than he did on the last two ...hen he came for his

THE MOST HUMAN OF PREMIERS

Sir Winston as the Commons Knows Him

BY HARRY BOARDMAN

"He loved England with the passionate enthusiasm which Pericles felt for Athens and he trusted the House of Commons as no one else. These words used of the heroic Sir John Eliot who withstood Charles I can be applied with a strict appropriateness to Winston Churchill.

For an adjective that so obviously and clearly expressed his own belief about the House.

As for trusting the House no more than an example of it could be found than his conduct during the war. Hardly a day passed when he was in London but he passed to his place...

For some time during this last spell in office as Prime Minister, people had been speculating privately or publicly as to how long Winston could keep going. Naturally the serious illness he had sustained in the summer of 1953 brought this question to the forefront, although he had made such a convincing comeback that autumn. At his best, Winston could still make a remarkable, indeed, a unique contribution: but it was all achieved with far greater expenditure of his effort and energy. He himself not only felt a natural reluctance finally to relinquish the reins of office, but he also had a deep conviction (not unfounded in reality) that he still had the capacity to influence events, especially in the field of world affairs. But as time went on he realized that his resignation as Prime Minister could not be indefinitely postponed, for Parliament was in its fourth year, and he knew he could not fight the next General Election as Prime Minister and Party Leader. And so the – for him infinitely painful – decision had to be taken. After much chopping and changing a date in early April 1955 was fixed. In all this, Clementine's attitude had been the same – *she* had never wanted Winston to continue in politics after 1945, let alone take on another stint as Prime Minister. 'Winston may not want to retire, but *I* do!' she would say ruefully. Not surprisingly, she was profoundly exhausted both physically and nervously by the sustained effort of these latter years, and in the Spring of 1955 she would celebrate her seventieth birthday. But she had loyally trudged on – although her heart was not in this last lap, and her health was indifferent all this time.

Tantalizingly, there was a strike in the newspaper industry from 25 March which lasted nearly a month. During this time there were no London national newspapers, but in the provinces the *Manchester Guardian* continued publication. It was ironic, therefore, that Winston Churchill's resignation, which was obviously of enormous interest, took place with the minimum of description or comment. Low's cartoon, with its muted trumpets and muffled drums, says it all!

Elizabeth R

1955.

Winston S. Churchill

April 4

On Monday 4 April, the Queen and the Duke of Edinburgh came to dine at No. 10 with Winston and Clementine. There was a splendid party of about fifty people – partly family, partly political, partly 'should auld acquaintance be forgot'. We all knew that this was a graceful, debonair farewell – but no one referred to it. It was a poignant moment for Winston, and we all felt it deeply for him.

In this charming and touching photograph, Winston is taking leave of Her Majesty on the doorstep of No. 10. The next day he presided at his last Cabinet meeting, and in the afternoon he went to Buckingham Palace and tendered his resignation to the Queen. And then he drove down to Chartwell.

Twilight and evening bell

399   Sarah Churchill

After his resignation in 1955, Winston took some little time to revive in spirits – the stimulus to life had been removed. The difference between being 'in' or 'out' of office is dramatic even in more lowly appointments than that of Prime Minister; and the process of adjusting to a slower pace, and of not being at the hub of events brings its own 'withdrawal symptoms'. But gradually Winston's sense of enjoyment returned: painting, as ever, remained the most constant companion of his long leisure. Friends and family rallied round: he went even more now to the South of France, and stayed for longer periods, for there was no need to hurry back anymore. Of his newer diversions, racing afforded him many hours of pleasure – and moments of excitement when he witnessed the victories his horses achieved for him. Nor was he idle on the book front: *The History of the English Speaking Peoples* had been on the stocks for many years, giving way to more urgent priorities – now Winston spent many hours revising the draft of the four volumes of this uneven, but vivid and panoramic view of history. Honours were still accorded him – culminating in the conferment of Honorary Citizenship of the United States of America in 1963. But the accolade which warmed him most was the love, gratitude and admiration, which even now in his old age and retirement, continued to reach him from ordinary men and women throughout the world. The sketch above was drawn by Sarah in the late 1950s.

400

Winston passed many contented hours in the studio at Chartwell, which is at the bottom of the orchard. The walls, as you can see, were veritably 'papered' with his canvases.

401

But if Winston Churchill was now retired (although it must be remembered he remained a Member of Parliament until 1964),he most certainly was not forgotten! – and the path to Chartwell was well worn by the feet of faithful friends and former colleagues. In June 1956 the former President of the United States of America Mr Truman, with his wife, came to luncheon at Chartwell. Here is the luncheon party lined up on the front doorstep. Left to right: Mary; Sarah; Mrs Truman; Winston; Mr Truman; Clementine; Lord Beaverbrook; Christopher Soames.

402

Although Winston had never shone as a scholar in his schooldays, and he had never regarded them as 'the happiest days of his life' – yet the famous Harrow School Songs formed a strong nostalgic link for him with his old school. Unlike many boarding schools Harrow, although so near London, did not evacuate to a quieter and safer place. School numbers dropped to as low as 200 – but they stuck it out on 'the Hill'. In 1940 Winston had gone to the annual 'Songs Concert' for the first time since leaving the school, and so much enjoyed singing the famous songs once more, and being surrounded by eager young faces, that he took to going back to his old school every year, and hardly missed one 'Songs' for the rest of his life. This picture was taken when he visited the school in 1952.

Winston and Clementine both took great pleasure in being surrounded by their family of all ages, and there was hardly a summer weekend at Chartwell without visiting children and grandchildren. The swimming pool was a great attraction, and the tennis court had been turned into a croquet lawn, and many were the matches between mixed generations. Clementine was an 'ace' at croquet, and much enjoyed teaching the younger grandchildren to wield a mallet. Here (above left), she is playing with Celia Sandys (aged fifteen) in 1958.

Winston was not a croquet-player, but he enjoyed watching, sometimes supplying tactical advice. In this picture (top right), he seems to have acquired a collection of feathers, no doubt while on his regular tours of the lakes to feed his goldfish, the black swans and other sundry waterfowl. The tours also included visits to the cowshed and the pig-styes. The pigs enjoyed having their backs scratched. Winston commented: 'I like pigs: cats look down on human beings, dogs look up to them, but pigs just treat us as their equals'.

Winston and Clementine both enjoyed playing bezique and backgammon – these were the 'house' games; although 'Oklahoma' and gin rummy both had a period of favour just after the war. Here Winston is playing bezique at Blenheim, with Mary, Duchess of Marlborough (wife of the tenth Duke). Winston's close ties with a younger generation of cousins continued throughout his life.

406

In 1958, Winston and Clementine celebrated their Golden Wedding. The world sent messages: their children gave them a Golden Rose Border at Chartwell. And, some centuries earlier, William Shakespeare had written a sonnet that could well have been dedicated to them.

This charming photograph, which for me epitomizes my parent's long and loving dialogue, was taken in the 1950s by the late Emery Reves who, with his wife Wendy, showed Winston and Clementine great hospitality at their beautiful house La Pausa, at Roquebrune, in the south of France.

Let me not to the marriage of true minds
Admit impediments. Love is not love
Which alters when it alteration finds,
Or bends with the remover to remove:
O, no! it is an ever-fixed mark,
That looks on tempests, and is never shaken;
It is the star to every wand'ring bark,
Whose worth's unknown, although his height be taken.
Love's not Time's fool, though rosy lips and cheeks
Within his bending sickle's compass come;
Love alters not with his brief hours and weeks,
But bears it out even to the edge of doom.
  If this be error, and upon me proved,
  I never writ, nor no man ever loved.

It was also in 1958 that Winston and Clementine went for the first of several cruises with the Greek millionaire shipowner, Aristotle Onassis and his beautiful and charming wife, Tina. Earlier that year Winston had been seriously ill with pneumonia, and now with hindsight, one realises that this illness marked a turning point from which his health and strength began a gentle, but inexorable decline. Formerly it had been Clementine who had so greatly enjoyed sea voyages: now Winston too found this new form of holiday both restful and pleasant. Winston was an honoured and welcome guest wherever the yacht *Christina* put into port, and crowds would quickly gather to greet him. This photograph was taken in 1960 when the *Christina* was lying off Split, on the Yugoslavian coast: President Tito and his wife came on board to pay their respects to one who had championed their cause in harder times. Left to right: Winston; President Tito; Ari Onassis; Madame Tito; Clementine.

I love this photograph of my father and my husband, taken at La Pausa when we were all guests of Emery and Wendy Reves. The friendship and affection between the so much older and the younger man were indeed touching to behold: and this relationship was an enrichment to both. Winston's influence on Christopher(coming at a moment in his life when, after his war service, he was turning to politics) was formative and crucial to his whole career. Christopher in his turn was able, as time went on, to render many services to his father-in-law. As their friendship matured, so did Winston's trust grow in Christopher, who became a constant companion, and a valued confidant and counsellor in affairs both public and private.

409

4

After Sarah and Antony Beauchamp had parted in 1955, she continued with her stage and screen career. But life was lonely for her, albeit amid many people, and she was made deeply unhappy by Antony's death in 1957. But, to the great joy of all of us who loved her, in 1962 she met, and a few months later married, a charming and gifted man, Henry Audley (23rd Baron Audley). Sarah was forty-eight and Henry nearly fifty. The family took to him at once: it all seemed perfect. But Sarah's newfound happiness was not destined to last: only fifteen months after their marriage, in July 1963, Henry died very suddenly from a massive coronary, in Spain where they were living.

Only a few months after Henry Audley's sudden death, another tragedy struck our family. Diana took her own life: she was fifty-four. After nearly twenty-five years of marriage with Duncan Sandys, they had been divorced in 1960. Diana had for some years suffered periods of nervous ill-health, and had known much torment and unhappiness. Yet, in the last months of her life, she had seemed calmer and happier: it was a tragic mystery. This photograph (above right) was taken on a sunshine, happy day, a few years earlier: 'Goodbye – for the present . . .'

411

In the summer of 1964 there was a joyous family event – young Winston (now twenty-four) married a charming girl, Minnie d'Erlanger. His grandfather was not up to going to the wedding or the reception, but the whole wedding party came to visit him at 28 Hyde Park Gate after the ceremony. Here is a family line-up, taken in the garden. Back row, left to right: Mrs Marion Martin; Leland Hayward (Pamela Churchill's husband); Mrs Penny Wilson (Bride's sister); Robin d'Erlanger (Bride's brother); Mrs F. Sammut (Bride's grandmother); Pamela, Lady Digby (Bridegroom's grandmother); Lord Digby and Lady Digby (Bridegroom's uncle and aunt); Clementine; Mrs Leland Hayward (Pamela, Bridegroom's mother); Mary Soames; Douglas Wilson (Bride's brother-in-law). Front row, left to right: Lady d'Erlanger (Bride's mother); Randolph Churchill; the Bride; Winston; the Bridegroom; sitting on the ground, Arabella (Bridegroom's half sister).

Although in these last years Winston was slowly declining – yet his health was remarkable when one considered all he had been through and his mounting tally of years. To most people's astonishment he presented himself yet again for election at Woodford at the General Election of 1959. Clementine had always played a great part in the life of his constituency, and now she did the larger share of the campaigning: but his supporters were loyal and indulgent, and indeed Winston made several speeches, and toured the constituency with Clementine: it was the fifteenth campaign they had fought together. He rarely spoke in the House of Commons now, but he attended quite often, and both Members and visitors in the public galleries liked to see him in his familiar place. When he left the House for the last time in July 1964, he had been a Member of Parliament almost continuously for over half a century, and he had represented the same constituency for forty years. In June 1962, while staying in the Hotel de Paris in Monte Carlo, Winston fell down and broke his

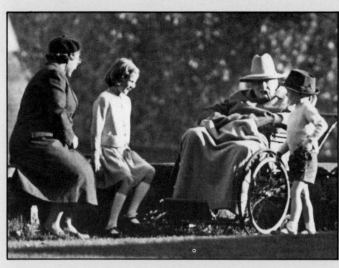

412

femur. He was flown home in an R.A.F. Comet, and was in the Middlesex Hospital for some six weeks before returning home. His health was still now a matter of touching concern to the general public, and even minor maladies and mishaps if reported by the press, touched off a stream of anxious enquiries: cards, letters, and even remedies, arriving by shoals through the post. Winston recovered slowly from this last accident, and his general mobility was considerably affected.

During the last summer at Chartwell, two of my children, Charlotte (aged ten) and Rupert (aged five) with their nannie, Miss Hilda King, are seen (above) talking to their grandfather. And now, in these last two years, the pace of life for Winston was very slow: it was like a broad, weary river, gently meandering on. Sometimes he seemed quite content: even though he might not say very much, one knew he was glad one was there. But sometimes he withdrew a great distance from us – and who knows what thoughts or images moved across the screen of his consciousness from the long saga of his life, so crowded with events and people? And, even now, Chartwell did not fail him: in the summer days he loved to sit out in his chair on the lawn, and gaze away across the valley and the lakes to the green and misty blue distances of the Weald. One felt he was at peace with himself and with the world:

'I warmed both hands before the fire
    of life;
It sinks, and I am ready to depart.'
(Walter Savage Landor)

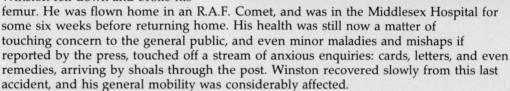

413

414

January 1965

415

For three days Winston Churchill lay in state in Westminster Hall, and 320,000 people waited for hours (by day and by night) in bitter weather to file through the great Hall to take their leave of one who had become a legend in his own lifetime. On Saturday 30 January, the funeral procession wound its long, magnificent way to St Paul's Cathedral, through streets lined by immense crowds of solemn, silent people. Below, the coffin is borne by Grenadier guardsmen into St Paul's, where a vast congregation was headed by the Queen who – waiving all custom and precedence – awaited the arrival of her greatest subject. Following behind the coffin are Clementine with Randolph, and other members of the close family.

417

The Funeral Service was unforgettable: the grandeur of the scene and the beauty of the singing; the blending of the imperishable language of our old Prayer Book with the familiar simplicity of well-loved hymns, wove a moving, splendid tapestry. Here, on the Cathedral steps, the Queen and members of the Royal Family watch as the coffin on its gun-carriage moves away. Behind the Queen and Prince Philip are seen the Queen Mother with Prince Charles (then a schoolboy); Princess Margaret and the Earl of Snowdon; the Duke and Duchess of Gloucester, and on the Duke's left, The Princess Royal (the Queen's Aunt).

Winston Churchill could have lain in Westminster Abbey or St Paul's Cathedral – but he wished to be buried in the churchyard of St Martin's, Bladon, the village church just outside the park walls of Blenheim. And so here – we his family – gathered in the dusk of that great day and laid him in the earth alongside his parents and kinsfolk, and within sight of the great house, where, ninety years before, he had been born.

418

Clementine alone

419

Although Winston's death had left Clementine bereft, yet coming after years of slow decline, there was no traumatic element of shock. Nevertheless, the sluggish pace of those twilight years had exacted its toll of her still lively personality; and the re-orientation of life after fifty years of devoted partnership, requires a little space. But Clementine remained a realist — nor did her courage desert her now. She did not linger long (she rarely had) over necessary decisions: Chartwell was promptly handed over to the National Trust, and Clementine took a great personal interest in the details of its rearrangement, giving to the Trust furniture, pictures and other treasured possessions, which ensured that Chartwell would not be merely a museum, but remain for posterity truly the home she and Winston and their family had inhabited for forty memorable years. Their London house, 28 Hyde Park Gate, was sold, and Clementine moved into a roomy, tree-top apartment in Prince's Gate, only a few blocks away. Gradually Clementine adapted to life, not so much *by* herself — as *for* herself, and a new and (on the whole pleasant) pattern of existence slowly took its shape; she cultivated old friends once more, and made some delightful new ones. As time went on, increasing deafness and failing eyesight were burdens she endured with stoicism; but the affection and respect afforded her by a wide public, and the loving concern of her family, were sources of satisfaction and joy to her.

On 1 April 1965, Clementine celebrated her eightieth birthday. We all gave her a luncheon party, and tried to make her feel surrounded with our love. In May she was delighted and truly gratified to have conferred upon her a Life Peerage. She took the title of Baroness Spencer-Churchill of Chartwell. On 15 June she took her seat with all due ceremony in the House of Lords: her sponsors were two faithful and trusted friends of Winston's – Lord Ismay ('Pug' of the war years) on the left of the picture and Lord Normanbrook (who as Sir Norman Brook had been secretary to the Cabinet during Winston's last prime ministership).

421

Very suddenly on 6 June 1968, Randolph died at Stour, his home in Suffolk: he was fifty-seven. Although his death was unexpected and a great shock, Randolph had, in fact, been in failing health since a lung operation in 1964. In 1960, Winston had entrusted to Randolph the task of writing his official biography; and from that time Randolph had concentrated all his powers on this mammoth work. By the time of his death, two volumes had been published, and a third was nearly completed: the work was thereafter taken over by Dr Martin Gilbert M.A. Winston loved (and as a child and youth had indulged) Randolph, whose love and loyalty to his father never faltered: but their relationship was one of storm and sunshine. Clementine realised that Winston spoilt Randolph, and encouraged in him higher expectations of what life would render him than were either wise or realistic. In maturity, Randolph and his mother were too different in temperament and outlook to give each other an easy time. But as the years rolled on, Randolph became more understanding of his mother. Latterly Clementine used to visit Randolph at Stour. After Winston's death, their relationship became smoother, and Clementine would often look to Randolph for support and counsel in various matters. In this sad picture, young Winston is escorting his grandmother to Randolph's Memorial Service in St Margaret's, Westminster. Clementine at eighty-three had buried three of her children: little Marigold; Diana; and now, Randolph.

422

In the Autumn of 1968, my husband Christopher was appointed British Ambassador to France: it was a great surprise, because Christopher is a politician, not a diplomat! At Victoria Station, were Christopher's mother Hope Dynevor, and my own, to see us off, and bid us 'God speed' on this exciting new assignment. Left to right: Hope, Lady Dynevor; Charlotte (aged fourteen), with Jim her pug-dog; myself; Christopher; my mother; Emma (aged nineteen) with Shingle, Christopher's beautiful black labrador.

423

In all these last years, Clementine continued to play her part as best she might in the world of public life of which, for so many years, both as Winston's wife and as herself, she had been a part. Now, perhaps, she could only make her formal *acte de presence* at the various ceremonies and functions – but as long as strength remained to her, she would do that.

One event she attended with regularity was the Service of Thanksgiving held yearly at Westminster Abbey to commemorate the Battle of Britain. She made a striking, dignified figure in black, with her row of medals. This picture was taken in 1967. Clementine attended this Service for the last time in 1976 – the year before she died: she was ninety-one. Now she could no longer manage the long walk up the aisle of the Abbey, and as she was pushed to her place in a wheel-chair, it was poignant and moving to see the congregation in the nave rise spontaneously to their feet.

424

But life for Clementine was not all being 'on parade': she now had leisure for friends and ploys and expeditions, which her long years of life with Winston had often crowded out. Clementine in her eighties was still open to new experiences, and in 1970 and 1971 she ventured on (for her) a new style of holiday – a voyage in a cruise liner. For a companion she took with her Nonie Chapman, her young secretary. Nonie had come to work for my mother in 1964, and was to be with her until her death; and it was largely due to Nonie that my mother had so much happiness and activity in these last years of her life. In September 1970, Clementine went for a Mediterranean/Atlantic cruise in the Royal Mail Lines' Ship *Andes*: she enjoyed herself very much, and took quite a part in shipboard life. She entered the Fancy Dress Competition as 'A Lady in Black' – and won first prize! Above in the front row 'A Lady in Black', and, second from the left, standing, Nonie Chapman representing 'An English Summer'!

425

On 1 April 1974, Clementine celebrated her eighty-ninth birthday. Christopher and I gave a luncheon party in her honour at Claridge's. Here she is cutting her birthday cake, watched by Edward Heath (one of the very few 'non-family' guests at our luncheon; he was a most faithful friend in these last years to my mother), and Lord Avon (Anthony Eden now, by his marriage to Winston's niece Clarissa, a member of the family as well as a friend).

426

The Winston Churchill Memorial Trust was founded after Winston's death. Thousands of people throughout Great Britain and the Commonwealth subscribed to the Trust which provides Travelling Fellowships which enable men and women from all walks of life and a wide age span to travel abroad and bring back knowledge and experience which enriches not only their own lives, but the community. The Memorial Trust thrives today, offering 100 Fellowships yearly in a number of categories which are changed annually. Every year or so there is a ceremony when Churchill Fellows receive commemorative medallions. In 1974, Prince Charles made the presentations in the Royal Festival Hall. Here the Prince is talking to Clementine and young Winston Churchill (author and journalist, and since 1970, a Conservative Member of Parliament) at the reception.

427

After Winston died, Clementine spent several Christmases with Christopher and me and our five children, at our home in Sussex. After we went to Paris, she came out to us there at Christmastime. From 1973 onwards Clementine spent Christmas with Winston and Minnie and their four children at Broadwater House, near Chailey in Sussex.
This photograph was taken by her nephew, Peregrine Churchill, in 1975, at Broadwater House. Standing: Yvonne Churchill, Peregrine's wife. In front of her, grouped round their great-grandmother: Marina (eight), Jennie (nine), Randolph (ten). 'Baby' Jack, born earlier that year, was not on view.

428

In 1974, there were a number of events to mark the centenary of Winston Churchill's birth in 1874, the most important and popular of which was a comprehensive and most beautifully devised Centenary Exhibition, housed in the State Rooms of Somerset House. One was taken back into the history of the Churchill family, and Winston's great ancestor, John, Duke of Marlborough, and then right through Winston's own wonderful life. Many of his own paintings were exhibited, as well as numerous items of Churchilliana, which intrigued, amused or interested the great throng of the public who, over a period of many weeks, visited the Exhibition. Queen Elizabeth, the Queen Mother, with customary grace and charm had opened the Exhibition on 9 May 1974, and this beautiful and evocative photograph of Clementine was taken on that occasion, when she was awaiting the arrival of Her Majesty. The bust of Winston, before which Clementine is seated, was executed by Oscar Nemon, who had sculpted Winston many times from life, and who always conveyed both his strength and grand humanity.

Clementine Churchill died at her home, very suddenly, on 12 December 1977: she was in her ninety-third year. Her ashes were laid in Winston's grave at Bladon. On 24 January 1978 – the thirteenth anniversary of Winston's death – a service of thanksgiving for her life was held in Westminster Abbey. Clementine was survived by two of her daughters, ten grandchildren and fourteen great-grandchildren.

429

This photograph was taken on 12 January 1977 at the christening of Clementine Sylvia Hambro, the daughter of our second daughter Charlotte, and Richard Hambro. It was a bitter winter's day, and the church was as cold as charity, but Clementine came to share in the baptism of her thirteenth great-grandchild – her namesake.

No family album really has an end: one volume is put aside to be followed by others, recording the doings of succeeding generations. So I shall close this part of *our* family's chronicle with a picture which makes me look back to time past with so much loving pride and thankfulness – and forward, with bright and brave hope.

Photo Acknowledgements

Some pictures are listed twice, once under the source of the picture and once under the copyright-holder.

MARY SOAMES COLLECTION 4, 7, 12, 13, 18, 20, 42, 53, 56, 57, 59, 67, 71, 81, 82, 84, 85, 91, 93, 94, 110, 111, 129, 136, 137, 138, 139, 140, 141, 142, 143, 146, 147, 148, 149, 152, 154, 156, 160, 163, 195, 197, 199, 200, 201, 203, 210, 217, 226, 240, 260, 262, 271, 284, 294, 295, 301, 318, 319, 355, 357, 382, 389, 401, 404, 406, 407, 408, 410, 412, 420, 421, 423, 425, 428

BARONESS SPENCER CHURCHILL COLLECTION (*Courtesy Sunday Times/ Thomson Trust*) 19, 22, 40, 41, 43, 44, 45, 46, 47, 48, 49, 50, 51, 52, 54, 66, 73, 75, 77, 78, 79, 87, 102, 103, 104, 115, 116, 117, 118, 127, 131, 134, 135, 206, 208, 212, 214, 215, 219, 227, 228, 229, 230, 233, 234, 238, 242, 243, 244, 246, 255, 257, 258, 259, 261, 266, 267, 268, 274, 275, 276, 277, 278, 279, 283, 285, 286, 298, 312, 314, 317, 327, 328, 330, 331, 336, 337, 338, 339, 342, 343, 346, 347, 373, 375, 383, 384, 392, 393, 394, 403, 424, 426

SARAH, LADY AUDLEY 207, 224, 326, 399, 409

THE RT. HON. THE LORD SOAMES G.C.M.G., G.C.V.O., C.H., C.B.E. 358, 398

PEREGRINE CHURCHILL 3, 6, 8, 15, 26, 62, 92, 99, 105, 107, 108, 109, 112, 133, 172, 205, 213, 231, 270, 329, 427

WINSTON S. CHURCHILL M.P. 124

HIS GRACE THE DUKE OF MARL- BOROUGH, BLENHEIM PALACE 2, 10, 11, 21, 31, 32, 33, 63, 64, 405

ASSOCIATED PRESS 173, 294, 360, 417, 423, 428

SPORT & GENERAL 90, 98, 349, 421

CECIL BEATON 200, 252, 260

BBC HULTON PICTURE LIBRARY 35, 96, 106, 119, 155, 157, 179, 220, 221, 235, 241, 249, 272, 291, 292, 296

ANTONY BEAUCHAMP 380

CAMERA PRESS 411

THE VISCOUNT CAMROSE 122, 123, 370

MRS THELMA CAZALET-KEIR 151

CENTRAL PRESS PHOTOS 196, 203, 239, 369, 402, 416, 422

PRESS PHOTOGRAPH COLLECTION, held by CHURCHILL COLLEGE, CAM- BRIDGE 86, 88, 90, 98, 126, 128, 150, 157, 159, 173, 175, 189, 198, 253, 321, 356, 360, 376, 380, 385, 402

BROADWATER COLLECTION, held by CHURCHILL COLLEGE, CAMBRIDGE 1, 5, 9, 14, 16, 23, 28, 36, 39, 89, 97, 121, 130, 153, 159, 164, 167, 168, 169, 170, 171, 174, 178, 180, 181, 184, 186, 187, 191, 216, 269, 313, 359, 362, 364, 368, 381

WILLIAM COLLINS SON & CO LTD 192

SIR JOHN COLVILLE C.B., C.V.O. 290

© **THE CONDÉ NAST PUBLICATIONS LTD. PHOTO A. DENNEY from HOUSE & GARDEN** 263

HOWARD COSTER 194

THE ADMINISTRATIVE TRUSTEES OF THE CHEQUERS ESTATE & H.M.S.O. 254, 256

DAILY GRAPHIC 69 (14 Sep 1908), 120 (6 Dec 1915)

DAILY HERALD 175

DAILY MAIL 223

DAILY TELEGRAPH 60 (25 Apr 1908)

DITCHLEY FOUNDATION 264

A. EISENSTAEDT, LIFE © **TIME INC./ COLORIFIC** 378

EUROPEAN PICTURE SERVICE 113

SYNDICS OF THE FITZWILLIAM MUSEUM, CAMBRIDGE 76

FOX PHOTOS LTD 245, 265, 301, 386, 392

THE JOHN FROST HISTORICAL NEWS- PAPER COLLECTION 58 (Daily Mirror, 15 Aug 1908), 70 (Daily Mirror, 14 Sep 1908), 126A (The Globe, 11 Nov 1918), 162 (British Gazette No. 8, May 1926), 222 (Daily Ex- press, 12 Dec 1936), 237 (Sunday Pictorial, 23 Apr 1939), 247 (News Chronicle, 5 June 1940), 248 (Sunday Dispatch, 23 June 1940), 250 (Daily Sketch, 19 Aug 1940), 297 (Daily Mail, 8 Dec 1941), 307, 310A (Sunday Dis- patch, 8 Dec 1945), 333 (The Star, 6 June 1944), 345 (Daily Telegraph, 8 May 1945), 348 (Daily Telegraph, 9 May 1945), 350 (Daily Mirror, 8 May 1950), 354 (Daily Mail, 27 Sep 1945), 377 (Evening Standard, 26 Oct 1951), 387 (The Observer, 28 June 1953), 413 (Evening Standard, 15 Jan 1965), 414 (Daily Telegraph, 25 Jan 1965)

MAJOR-GENERAL SIR EDMUND HAKE- WILL-SMITH 114

© **PHILIPPE HALSMAN** 358

HAMLYN PUBLISHING GROUP LTD 188

HARPERS 1900 27

THE VISCOUNTESS HEAD 390, 391

HODDER & STOUGHTON LTD 38

ILLUSTRATED LONDON NEWS 17 (24 Sep 1898), 24 (The Sketch, 1 Aug 1900), 25 (The Sketch, 1 Aug 1900), 61 (9 May 1908), 65 (The Sketch, 9 Sep 1908), 68 (12 Sep 1908), 80, 83, 95 (The Sphere, 4 Oct 1913), 101, 125 (The Sketch, 5 June 1918), 161, 185, 202, 218 (and jacket), 225, 251, 287, 305 (The Sphere, 7 Nov 1942), 306 (The Sphere, 7 Nov 1942), 352, 369, 374

TRUSTEES OF THE IMPERIAL WAR MUSEUM, LONDON 236, 273, 280, 281, 288, 289, 293, 299, 300, 302, 303, 304, 308, 309, 310, 315, 316, 320, 322, 323, 324, 332, 334, 335, 340, 341, 367

KEYSTONE PRESS AGENCY 74, 311, 352, 361, 371, 372, 379, 388, 395, 418, 429

LONDON EXPRESS NEWS AND FEATURE SERVICES 410, 420

LONDON NEWS AGENCY 156

THE LOW TRUSTEES AND THE LONDON EVENING STANDARD 282, 325, 397

MANCHESTER GUARDIAN 396

PAUL MAZE (Dec'd) 238

MINISTRY OF DEFENCE 419

NATIONAL MARITIME MUSEUM 100

NATIONAL TRUST, CHARTWELL Fron- tispiece, 132, 144, 145, 190, 209, 211, 363

PHOTOGRAPHIC NEWS AGENCIES 253

POPPERFOTO 189, 193, 198, 351, 385

PORTMAN PRESS BUREAU 366

PRESS ASSOCIATION 72, 204, 415

EMERY REVES (Dec'd) 406, 408

MICHAEL ROSS-WILLS 190, 211

MARY, DUCHESS OF ROXBURGHE 34

SOTHEBY'S LONDON 252

SUNDAY TIMES 407

SUNDAY TIMES/THOMSON TRUST 383, 384

SYNDICATION INTERNATIONAL 158, 237, 307, 350

D C THOMSON 146

THE TIMES 55, 286

TOPICAL PRESS AGENCY 88, 150

TOWN & COUNTRY NEWS 207, 208

HUGO VICKERS 29, 30, 37, 165, 166, 176, 177, 182, 183

VIVIENNE 375

HANS WILD, LIFE © **1946 TIME INC./ COLORIFIC** 400

ZOOLOGICAL SOCIETY OF LONDON 232

PENGUIN BOOKS

A CHURCHILL FAMILY ALBUM

Mary Soames was born in 1922, the youngest of Winston and Clementine Churchill's five children. She was brought up at Chartwell, attending a local private school as a day-pupil until 1939. During the first two years of the war she worked for the Red Cross and the W.V.S., and in 1941 she joined the A.T.S. She served in mixed anti-aircraft batteries, mainly in the United Kingdom, but also in Belgium and Germany, rising through the ranks to a commission and the eventual rank of Junior Commander. She also accompanied her father on several of his overseas journeys, acting as his A.D.C.

Demobilized in 1946, she married Captain Christopher Soames of the Coldstream Guards, who was at that time Assistant Military Attaché in Paris. After leaving the army he became Conservative M.P. for Bedford from 1950 to 1966, and Mary Soames campaigned with her husband at six elections. Having held several government posts and attained Cabinet rank, Christopher Soames was sent to Paris as British Ambassador, where he and his wife and family lived from 1968 to 1972. In 1973, Sir Christopher was appointed first British Vice-President of the European Commission, and until 1976 he and Lady Soames lived in Brussels. From December 1979 to April 1980 Lady Soames accompanied her husband on his appointment as the last British Governor of Southern Rhodesia. Lord and Lady Soames have five children.

Mary Soames was United Kingdom Chairman of the International Year of the Child in 1979; she is a member of the Council of the Winston Churchill Memorial Trust; a Governor of Harrow School, and an Honorary Fellow of Churchill College, Cambridge. In 1980 she was made a Dame Commander of the Order of the British Empire. She likes reading, travelling and sightseeing and – above all – family life, living in the country and gardening. Mary Soames is also author of *Clementine Churchill*, the best-selling biography of her mother, which won a Wolfson History Prize and the *Yorkshire Post* Prize for Best First Work in 1979.

A
CHURCHILL
FAMILY ALBUM

A personal anthology selected by
MARY SOAMES

PENGUIN BOOKS

Penguin Books Ltd, Harmondsworth, Middlesex, England
Viking Penguin Inc., 40 West 23rd Street, New York, New York 10010, U.S.A.
Penguin Books Australia Ltd, Ringwood, Victoria, Australia
Penguin Books Canada Ltd, 2801 John Street, Markham, Ontario, Canada L3R 1B4
Penguin Books (N.Z.) Ltd, 182–190 Wairau Road, Auckland 10, New Zealand

First published by Allen Lane 1982
Published in Penguin Books 1985

Made and printed in Great Britain by Lund Humphries Ltd, Bradford
Typeset in Palatino

Frontispiece

Winston and Clementine Churchill at Chartwell:
the sketch for the conversation piece by William Nicholson,
commissioned by a group of their friends
to mark their Silver Wedding in 1933. The picture hangs at Chartwell.